PRISM READING

Student's Book

2

Lida Baker
Carolyn Westbrook
with
Christina Cavage

CAMBRIDGE
UNIVERSITY PRESS

University Printing House, Cambridge CB2 8BS, United Kingdom

One Liberty Plaza, 20th Floor, New York, NY 10006, USA

477 Williamstown Road, Port Melbourne, VIC 3207, Australia

314–321, 3rd Floor, Plot 3, Splendor Forum, Jasola District Centre, New Delhi – 110025, India

79 Anson Road, #06–04/06, Singapore 079906

Cambridge University Press is part of the University of Cambridge.

It furthers the University's mission by disseminating knowledge in the pursuit of
education, learning and research at the highest international levels of excellence.

www.cambridge.org
Information on this title: www.cambridge.org/9781108622004

First published 2018
20 19 18 17 16 15 14 13 12 11 10 9 8 7 6 5 4 3 2 1

Printed in Malaysia by Vivar

A catalogue record for this publication is available from the British Library

ISBN 978-1-108-62200-4 Prism Reading 2 Student's Book with Online Workbook
ISBN 978-1-108-45531-2 Prism Reading 2 Teacher's Manual

CONTENTS

SCOPE AND SEQUENCE

UNIT	READING PASSAGES	KEY READING SKILLS	ADDITIONAL READING SKILLS
1 ANIMALS *Academic Disciplines* Ecology / Zoology	1 Endangered Species (article) 2 Losing the Battle for Survival (article)	Reading for main ideas Using a Venn diagram	Understanding key vocabulary Using your knowledge Reading for details Working out meaning Predicting content using visuals Taking notes Summarizing Making inferences Synthesizing
2 THE ENVIRONMENT *Academic Disciplines* Environmental Science / Natural Science	1 Our Changing Planet (web page) 2 The Causes and Effects of Deforestation (article)	Reading for details Taking notes on causes and effects	Understanding key vocabulary Predicting content using visuals Reading for main ideas Scanning to find information Identifying purpose Previewing Summarizing Making inferences Synthesizing
3 TRANSPORTATION *Academic Disciplines* Transportation Management / Urban Planning	1 Masdar: the Future of Cities? (case study) 2 A reading about traffic congestion (essay)	Predicting content using visuals	Understanding key vocabulary Reading for main ideas Reading for details Making inferences Taking notes Synthesizing
4 CUSTOMS AND TRADITIONS *Academic Disciplines* Cultural Studies / Sociology	1 Customs around the World (article) 2 Nontraditional Weddings (online article)	Annotating	Understanding key vocabulary Using your knowledge Taking notes Reading for main ideas Making inferences Previewing Reading for details Synthesizing

LANGUAGE DEVELOPMENT	WATCH AND LISTEN	SPECIAL FEATURES
Academic verbs Comparative adjectives	Animal Teamwork	Critical Thinking Collaboration
Academic vocabulary Environment collocations	The Role of Water in U.S. Natural Wonders	Critical Thinking Collaboration
Transportation collocations Synonyms for verbs	The Jumbo Jet	Critical Thinking Collaboration
Avoiding generalizations Adverbs of frequency to avoid generalizations Synonyms to avoid generalizations	Halloween by the Numbers	Critical Thinking Collaboration

UNIT	READING PASSAGES	KEY READING SKILLS	ADDITIONAL READING SKILLS
5 HEALTH AND FITNESS *Academic Disciplines* Medicine / Nutrition	1 A reading about health and exercise (article) 2 Tackling Obesity (essay)	Making inferences	Understanding key vocabulary Predicting content using visuals Skimming Reading for main ideas Reading for details Using your knowledge Scanning to predict content Taking notes Synthesizing
6 DISCOVERY AND INVENTION *Academic Disciplines* Industrial Design / Mechanical Engineering	1 The Magic of Mimicry (article) 2 Technology of the Future (online article)	Scanning to find information Using a T-chart	Understanding key vocabulary Previewing Reading for main ideas Annotating Making inferences Using your knowledge Taking notes Reading for details Synthesizing
7 FASHION *Academic Disciplines* Fashion Design / Retail Management	1 Is Fast Fashion Taking Over? (online article) 2 Offshore Textile Production: Why It Must Change (essay)	Distinguishing fact from opinion	Understanding key vocabulary Using your knowledge Reading for main ideas Reading for details Making inferences Skimming Scanning to find information Taking notes Synthesizing
8 ECONOMICS *Academic Disciplines* Business / Economics	1 Investing: Two Alternatives to Consider (article) 2 What Has Happened to the American Dream? (online article)	Skimming Understanding line graphs	Understanding key vocabulary Using your knowledge Reading for main ideas Reading for details Making inferences Scanning to find information Annotating Taking notes Synthesizing

LANGUAGE DEVELOPMENT	WATCH AND LISTEN	SPECIAL FEATURES
Verb and noun forms Health and fitness collocations	Nutrition Labels	Critical Thinking Collaboration
Making predictions with modals and adverbs of certainty Prefixes	China's Man-made River	Critical Thinking Collaboration
Vocabulary for the fashion business	A Life Tailored Around Clothes	Critical Thinking Collaboration
Nouns and adjectives for economics Nouns for economic trends	The Stock Market Crash of 1929	Critical Thinking Collaboration

1 READING

Receptive, language, and analytical skills
Students improve their reading skills through a sequence of proven activities. First they study key vocabulary to prepare for each reading and to develop academic reading skills. Then they work on synthesis exercises in the second reading that prepare students for college classrooms. Language Development sections teach vocabulary, collocations, and language structure.

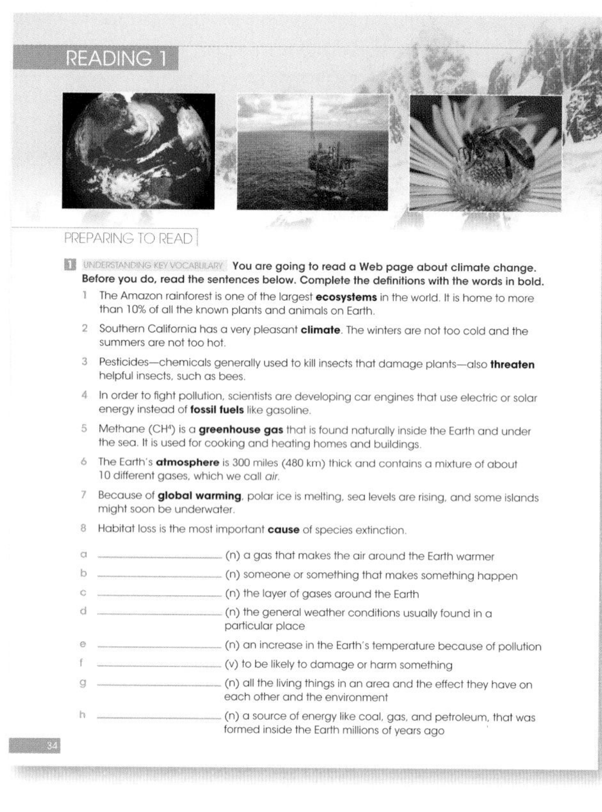

READING 1

PREPARING TO READ

1 UNDERSTANDING KEY VOCABULARY **You are going to read a Web page about climate change. Before you do, read the sentences below. Complete the definitions with the words in bold.**

1 The Amazon rainforest is one of the largest **ecosystems** in the world. It is home to more than 10% of all the known plants and animals on Earth.
2 Southern California has a very pleasant **climate**. The winters are not too cold and the summers are not too hot.
3 Pesticides—chemicals generally used to kill insects that damage plants—also **threaten** helpful insects, such as bees.
4 In order to fight pollution, scientists are developing car engines that use electric or solar energy instead of **fossil fuels** like gasoline.
5 Methane (CH^4) is a **greenhouse gas** that is found naturally inside the Earth and under the sea. It is used for cooking and heating homes and buildings.
6 The Earth's **atmosphere** is 300 miles (480 km) thick and contains a mixture of about 10 different gases, which we call *air*.
7 Because of **global warming**, polar ice is melting, sea levels are rising, and some islands might soon be underwater.
8 Habitat loss is the most important **cause** of species extinction.

a ______________ (n) a gas that makes the air around the Earth warmer
b ______________ (n) someone or something that makes something happen
c ______________ (n) the layer of gases around the Earth
d ______________ (n) the general weather conditions usually found in a particular place
e ______________ (n) an increase in the Earth's temperature because of pollution
f ______________ (v) to be likely to damage or harm something
g ______________ (n) all the living things in an area and the effect they have on each other and the environment
h ______________ (n) a source of energy like coal, gas, and petroleum, that was formed inside the Earth millions of years ago

34

The Upsala glacier in Argentina used to be one of the biggest glaciers in South America. In 1928, it was covered in ice and snow, but now the glacier is melting at an annual rate of about 650 feet (about 200 meters), so the area is covered in water. This is evidence of global warming.

Effects of Climate Change

1 In the last 100 years, the global temperature has gone up by around 1.33°F (0.75°C). This may not sound like much, but such a small increase is causing sea levels to rise and **threatening** the habitat of many species of plants and animals. An increase of 3.6°F (2°C) in global temperatures could result in extinction for 30% of the world's land species.

2 The Northwest Passage is a sea route that runs along the northern coast of Canada between the Atlantic and the Pacific Oceans. In the past, it was often difficult to use because the water was frozen; however, increasing temperatures and the subsequent deglaciation[1] have made it easier for ships to travel through this route. The trouble is that the melting of the ice will lead to loss of habitat for the polar bears and other species that live in this area.

3 Experts predict that global sea levels could rise by 12 to 48 inches (30.5 to 122 centimeters) by the end of the century. Consequently, some areas that were land a few hundred years ago are now underwater, and many low-lying islands may be underwater in the future.

4 As a result of the changing **climate**, the world's **ecosystems** are also changing faster than ever before. More than one-third of the world's mangrove forests[2] and around 20% of the world's coral reefs[3] have been destroyed in the last few decades. Forests are being cut down to provide land for food, because human population is growing at such a rapid rate. Approximately a quarter of the land on Earth is now used for growing food. As a result of the higher temperatures and higher levels of carbon dioxide in the **atmosphere**, plants are producing more pollen, which could lead to more cases of asthma, a medical condition that makes it hard to breathe.

Causes of Climate Change

5 What is causing climate change? The main **cause** is the huge amount of **greenhouse gases**, such as methane and carbon dioxide (CO_2), in the atmosphere, but the reason for the high levels is the world's population—you and I. As the population increases, more land is needed to provide food and energy. Burning **fossil fuels** for heating, lighting, transportation, electricity, or manufacturing produces CO_2. Furthermore, humans breathe out CO_2 while trees "breathe in" CO_2 and produce oxygen, so by cutting down trees, we are increasing the amount of CO_2 in the atmosphere and reducing the amount of oxygen. As a result of human activities, CO_2 levels are now at their highest in 800,000 years.

What Can Be Done

6 The biggest challenge we all face is to prevent further environmental disasters. We must do something before it is too late. We need to reduce the amount of CO_2 in the atmosphere. We need to stop burning fossil fuels and start using renewable energy. We can get enough energy from renewable fuels such as solar energy, hydroelectric energy, or wind power to be able to stop using fossil fuels completely.

Click here to sign the petition to tell governments to take action before it is too late!

[1] **deglaciation** (n) the melting of a glacier
[2] **mangrove forests** (n) large areas of trees and shrubs that live in coastal areas, e.g., in Florida and Bangladesh
[3] **coral reefs** (n) diverse underwater ecosystems built by tiny animals

36 37

2 MORE READING

Critical thinking and collaboration

Multiple critical thinking activities prepare students for exercises that focus on academic reading skills. Collaboration activities help develop higher-level thinking skills, oral communication, and understanding of different opinions. By working with others students, they become better prepared for real life social and academic situations.

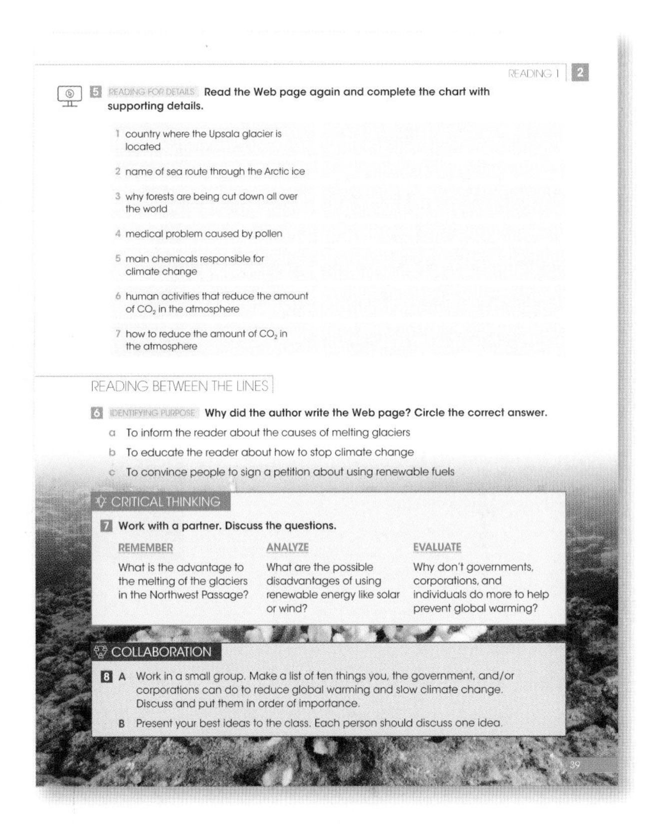

READING 1 | 2

5 READING FOR DETAILS Read the Web page again and complete the chart with supporting details.

1 country where the Upsala glacier is located
2 name of sea route through the Arctic ice
3 why forests are being cut down all over the world
4 medical problem caused by pollen
5 main chemicals responsible for climate change
6 human activities that reduce the amount of CO_2 in the atmosphere
7 how to reduce the amount of CO_2 in the atmosphere

READING BETWEEN THE LINES

6 IDENTIFYING PURPOSE Why did the author write the Web page? Circle the correct answer.

a To inform the reader about the causes of melting glaciers
b To educate the reader about how to stop climate change
c To convince people to sign a petition about using renewable fuels

CRITICAL THINKING

7 Work with a partner. Discuss the questions.

REMEMBER	ANALYZE	EVALUATE
What is the advantage to the melting of the glaciers in the Northwest Passage?	What are the possible disadvantages of using renewable energy like solar or wind?	Why don't governments, corporations, and individuals do more to help prevent global warming?

COLLABORATION

8 A Work in a small group. Make a list of ten things you, the government, and/or corporations can do to reduce global warming and slow climate change. Discuss and put them in order of importance.

B Present your best ideas to the class. Each person should discuss one idea.

39

3 VIDEO

Summarizing the unit

Each unit ends with a carefully selected video clip that piques student interest and pulls together what they have learned. Video lessons also develop key skills such as prediction, comprehension, and discussion.

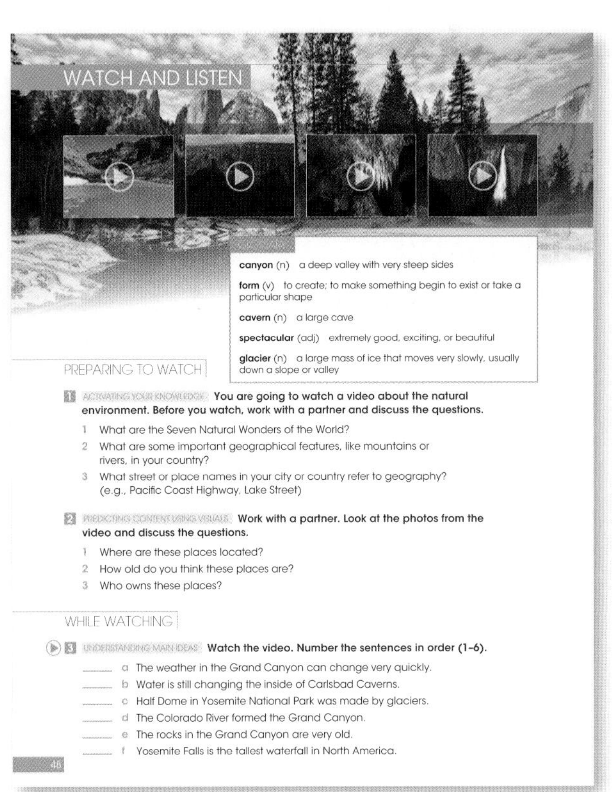

WATCH AND LISTEN

GLOSSARY

canyon (n) a deep valley with very steep sides
form (v) to create; to make something begin to exist or take a particular shape
cavern (n) a large cave
spectacular (adj) extremely good, exciting, or beautiful
glacier (n) a large mass of ice that moves very slowly, usually down a slope or valley

PREPARING TO WATCH

1 ACTIVATING YOUR KNOWLEDGE You are going to watch a video about the natural environment. Before you watch, work with a partner and discuss the questions.

1 What are the Seven Natural Wonders of the World?
2 What are some important geographical features, like mountains or rivers, in your country?
3 What street or place names in your city or country refer to geography? (e.g., Pacific Coast Highway, Lake Street)

2 PREDICTING CONTENT USING VISUALS Work with a partner. Look at the photos from the video and discuss the questions.

1 Where are these places located?
2 How old do you think these places are?
3 Who owns these places?

WHILE WATCHING

3 UNDERSTANDING MAIN IDEAS Watch the video. Number the sentences in order (1–6).

____ a The weather in the Grand Canyon can change very quickly.
____ b Water is still changing the inside of Carlsbad Caverns.
____ c Half Dome in Yosemite National Park was made by glaciers.
____ d The Colorado River formed the Grand Canyon.
____ e The rocks in the Grand Canyon are very old.
____ f Yosemite Falls is the tallest waterfall in North America.

48

PREPARE YOUR STUDENTS TO SUCCEED IN COLLEGE CLASSES AND BEYOND

Capturing interest

- Students experience the topics and expand their vocabulary through captivating readings and videos that pull together everything they have learned in the unit, while developing academic reading and critical thinking skills.
- Teachers can deliver effective and engaging lessons using Presentation Plus.

UNIT 2

THE ENVIRONMENT

Key Reading Skills	Reading for details; taking notes on causes and effects
Additional Reading Skills	Understanding key vocabulary; predicting content using visuals; reading for main ideas; scanning to find information; identifying purpose; previewing; summarizing; making inferences; synthesizing
Language Development	Academic vocabulary; environment collocations

ACTIVATE YOUR KNOWLEDGE

Work with a partner. Discuss the questions.

1 Is the weather changing in your country? How?
2 What are some ways that humans have affected the environment?
3 What is the biggest environmental problem in your country?

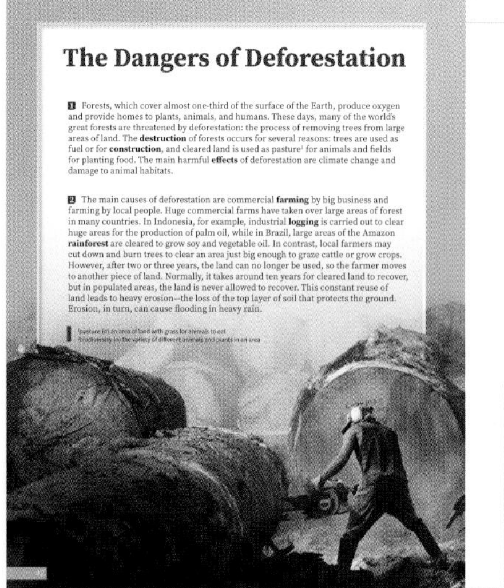

The Dangers of Deforestation

1 Forests, which cover almost one-third of the surface of the Earth, produce oxygen and provide homes to plants, animals, and humans. These days, many of the world's great forests are threatened by deforestation: the process of removing trees from large areas of land. The **destruction** of forests occurs for several reasons: trees are used as fuel or for **construction**, and cleared land is used as pasture[1] for animals and fields for planting food. The main harmful **effects** of deforestation are climate change and damage to animal habitats.

2 The main causes of deforestation are commercial **farming** by big business and farming by local people. Huge commercial farms have taken over large areas of forest in many countries. In Indonesia, for example, industrial **logging** is carried out to clear huge areas for the production of palm oil, while in Brazil, large areas of the Amazon **rainforest** are cleared to grow soy and vegetable oil. In contrast, local farmers may cut down and burn trees to clear an area just big enough to graze cattle or grow crops. However, after two or three years, the land can no longer be used, so the farmer moves to another piece of land. Normally, it takes around ten years for cleared land to recover, but in populated areas, the land is never allowed to recover. This constant reuse of land leads to heavy erosion—the loss of the top layer of soil that protects the ground. Erosion, in turn, can cause flooding in heavy rain.

[1]pasture (n) an area of land with grass for animals to eat
[2]biodiversity (n) the variety of different animals and plants in an area

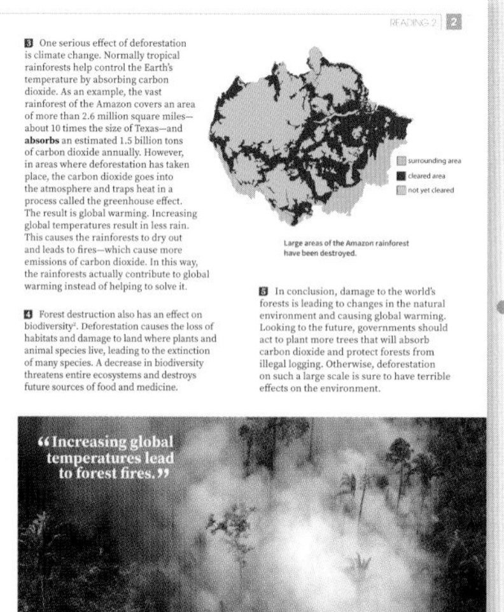

READING 2 | 2

3 One serious effect of deforestation is climate change. Normally tropical rainforests help control the Earth's temperature by absorbing carbon dioxide. As an example, the vast rainforest of the Amazon covers an area of more than 2.6 million square miles—about 10 times the size of Texas—and **absorbs** an estimated 1.5 billion tons of carbon dioxide annually. However, in areas where deforestation has taken place, the carbon dioxide goes into the atmosphere and traps heat in a process called the greenhouse effect. The result is global warming. Increasing global temperatures result in less rain. This causes the rainforests to dry out and leads to fires—which cause more emissions of carbon dioxide. In this way, the rainforests actually contribute to global warming instead of helping to solve it.

Large areas of the Amazon rainforest have been destroyed.

4 Forest destruction also has an effect on biodiversity[2]. Deforestation causes the loss of habitats and damage to land where plants and animal species live, leading to the extinction of many species. A decrease in biodiversity threatens entire ecosystems and destroys future sources of food and medicine.

5 In conclusion, damage to the world's forests is leading to changes in the natural environment and causing global warming. Looking to the future, governments should act to plant more trees that will absorb carbon dioxide and protect forests from illegal logging. Otherwise, deforestation on such a large scale is sure to have terrible effects on the environment.

"Increasing global temperatures lead to forest fires."

Building confidence

- *Prism Reading* teaches skills that enable students to read, understand, and analyze university texts with confidence.
- Readings from a variety of academic disciplines in different formats (essays, articles, websites, etc.) expose and prepare students to comprehend real-life text they may face in or outside the classroom.

Extended learning

- The Online Workbook has one extra reading and additional practice for each unit. Automated feedback gives autonomy to students while allowing teachers to spend less time grading and more time teaching.

Research-based

- Topics, vocabulary, academic and critical thinking skills to build students' confidence and prepare them for college courses were shaped by conversations with teachers at over 500 institutions.
- Carefully selected vocabulary students need to be successful in college are based on the General Service List, the Academic Word List, and the Cambridge English Corpus.

PATH TO BETTER LEARNING

CLEAR LEARNING OBJECTIVES

Every unit begins with clear learning objectives.

RICH CONTENT

Highly visual unit openers with discussion questions are engaging opportunities for previewing unit themes.

SCAFFOLDED INSTRUCTION

Activities and tasks support the development of critical thinking skills.

CRITICAL THINKING

After reading, targeted questions help develop critical thinking skills. The questions range in complexity to prepare students for higher-level course work.

COLLABORATIVE GROUP WORK

Critical thinking is followed by collaborative tasks and activities for the opportunity to apply new skills. Tasks are project-based and require teamwork, research, and presentation. These projects are similar to ones in an academic program.

EXTENDED LEARNING OPPORTUNITIES

In-class projects and online activities extend learning beyond the textbook.

WHAT MAKES *PRISM READING* SPECIAL: CRITICAL THINKING

BLOOM'S TAXONOMY

Prism Reading prepares students for college coursework by explicitly teaching a full range of critical thinking skills. Critical thinking exercises appear in every unit of every level, organized according to the taxonomy developed by Benjamin Bloom.

Critical thinking exercises are highlighted in a special box and indicates which skills the students are learning.

CRITICAL THINKING

7 SYNTHESIZING **Work with a partner. Use information from Reading 1 and Reading 2 to answer the questions.**

UNDERSTAND

As the world's climate changes, which places will have too much water? Which places will become drier?

EVALUATE

How do both the melting of the glaciers and deforestation contribute to the extinction of species?

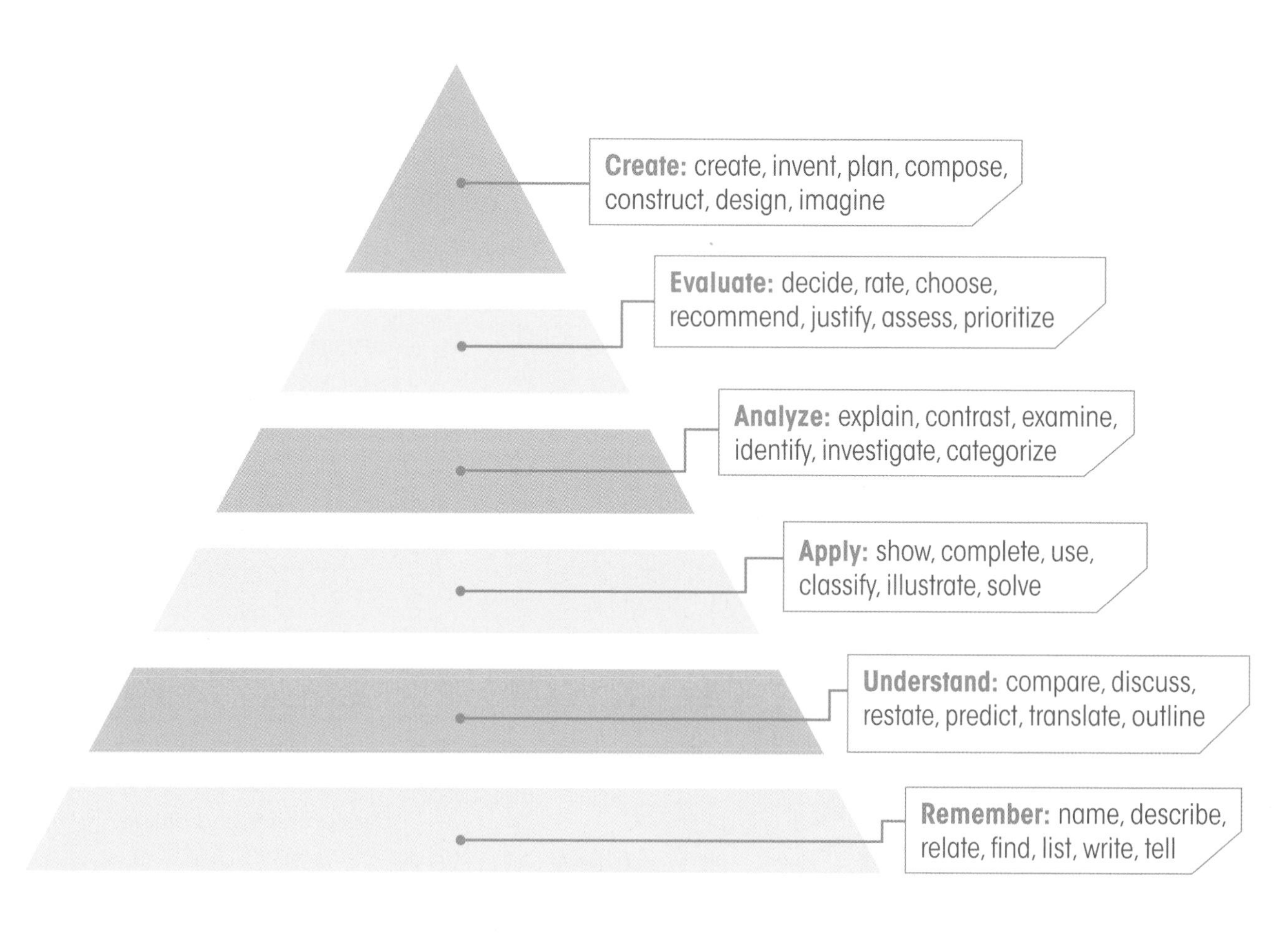

HIGHER-ORDER THINKING SKILLS

Create, Evaluate, Analyze

Students' academic success depends on their ability to derive knowledge from collected data, make educated judgments, and deliver insightful presentations. *Prism Reading* helps students gain these skills with activities that teach them the best solution to a problem, and develop arguments for a discussion or presentation.

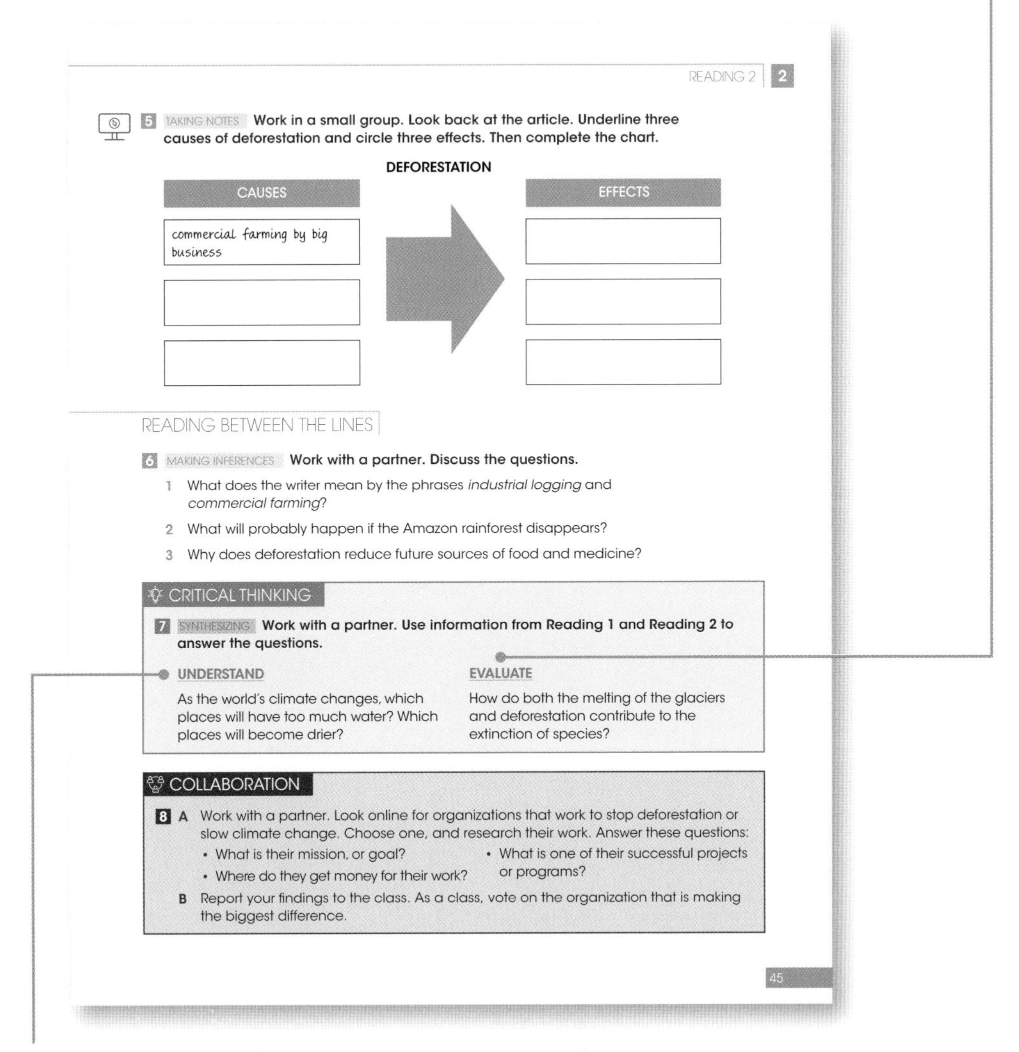

LOWER-ORDER THINKING SKILLS

Apply, Understand, Remember

Students need to be able to recall information, comprehend it, and see its use in new contexts. These skills form the foundation for all higher-order thinking, and *Prism Reading* develops them through exercises that teach note-taking, comprehension, and the ability to distill information from charts.

UNIT 1

ANIMALS

LEARNING OBJECTIVES	
Key Reading Skills	Reading for main ideas; using a Venn diagram
Additional Reading Skills	Understanding key vocabulary; using your knowledge; reading for details; working out meaning; predicting content using visuals; taking notes; summarizing; making inferences; synthesizing
Language Development	Academic verbs; comparative adjectives

ACTIVATE YOUR KNOWLEDGE

Work with a partner. Discuss the questions.

1 In your opinion, is it better to see animals in a zoo or in nature? Why?
2 Are there more wild animals in your country now, or were there more in the past? Why? Give examples.
3 Why do some people enjoy having animals in their homes?
4 Do humans need animals? Why or why not?
5 Are animals important in your life? Why?

READING 1

PREPARING TO READ

1 UNDERSTANDING KEY VOCABULARY **Read the definitions. Complete the sentences with the correct form of the words in bold.**

chemical (n) man-made or natural substance made by changing atoms
destroy (v) to damage something very badly; to cause it to not exist
due to (prep) because of; as a result of
endangered (adj) (of plants and animals) that may disappear soon
natural (adj) as found in nature; not made or caused by people
pollute (v) to make an area or substance dirty and unhealthful
protect (v) to keep something or someone safe from damage or injury
species (n) types of plants or animals that have similar features

1 The black rhino is one of the most ________________ animals in the world. There are only about 5,000 left today.
2 There are three ________________ of bears in North America. They are the American black bear, the grizzly bear, and the polar bear.
3 Dangerous ________________ from factories can kill fish and other animals when they enter lakes and rivers.
4 Smoke from factories can ________________ the air and hurt both humans and animals.
5 When new homes are built, it often ________________ the areas where animals live.
6 Few people visited the zoo last week ________________ the cold weather.
7 I don't like zoos. I prefer to see animals in their ________________ environments.
8 Many organizations are working to ________________ endangered animals by creating safe places for them to live.

2 USING YOUR KNOWLEDGE **Look at the title of the article on pages 18–19. What do you think it will be about? Complete the chart with the names of endangered and extinct species you know.**

ENDANGERED SPECIES	EXTINCT SPECIES

ENDANGERED SPECIES

1 An **endangered species** is a group of animals or plants that could soon become extinct. Extinction happens when the last animal of the species has died out and there will be no more. Many species are nearly extinct and could disappear from the Earth very soon if we don't do anything to save them. There are many reasons why species become endangered, but most harm to species is **due to** human activities such as habitat destruction, hunting, and overfishing.

2 Habitat destruction is the main reason why animals become endangered. This happens in two ways. First, when humans move into a new area, they cut down trees to build houses and farms. This **destroys** the animals' habitat—the **natural** environment where plants or animals usually live—and leaves them without food. Animal habitats are also destroyed because of pollution. Dirty water from factories, which contains **chemicals**, ends up in rivers, and poisons used on farmland may even kill animals that live in the area.

3 Endangered species are also the result of hunting and fishing. Animals such as the Arabian oryx are nearly extinct because of the high price of their meat. Other animals are killed for their fur, bones, or skin—or just for sport. For example, some seal species are now almost extinct because they are killed for their fur to make coats. Tigers are shot to make medicine and tea from their bones, and crocodiles are caught to make bags and shoes. Large sea creatures like whales, tuna, and sharks have all become endangered species because

What steps can individuals and governments take to protect more animal and plant species from becoming endangered?

Arabian oryx

of overfishing—too many are caught to make special dishes that people like to eat, such as shark's fin soup or sushi.

4 What steps can individuals and governments take to **protect** more animal and plant species from becoming endangered? We should try not to **pollute** natural areas, and farmers or companies who destroy animal habitats should face a financial penalty. The public can help out by refusing to buy products made from animals' body parts, such as seal fur coats or crocodile bags. Governments can help, too, by making it against the law to hunt, fish, or trade in endangered species. They can also provide funding for animal sanctuaries and zoos and protect animals from extinction by breeding more endangered animals, which can later be released into the wild. If we all cooperate by taking these steps, we will protect our planet so that our children and their children can enjoy it, too.

Tiger

Seal

Whale

WHILE READING

3 READING FOR DETAILS **Read the article on pages 18–19. Add the names of the animals mentioned to the correct column of the chart on page 17.**

SKILLS

READING FOR MAIN IDEAS

The main idea of a paragraph tells the most important thought or message of that paragraph. The topic sentence expresses the main idea of the paragraph, and all of the other sentences in the paragraph give details to support the topic sentence. To find the main idea, look at the topic sentence and check whether the rest of the paragraph supports what it says.

4 READING FOR MAIN IDEAS **Read the article again and write the paragraph number next to the main ideas.**

a How hunting and overfishing endanger animals ______

b The definition of endangered and extinct species ______

c How governments and citizens can protect animals ______

d How humans destroy and pollute animal habitats ______

5 READING FOR DETAILS **Work with a partner. Answer the questions.**

1 Who or what is most responsible for animal extinction and endangered species?

______

2 How does pollution and cutting down trees cause problems for animals?

______

3 What do people hunt animals for?

______

4 Which large sea creatures are endangered because of overfishing?

______

5 What can individuals do to protect animals from becoming endangered?

______

6 What should governments do about hunting and fishing of animals?

______

7 What should governments invest in to get more animals back into the wild?

______

READING BETWEEN THE LINES

6 WORKING OUT MEANING **Read the last paragraph of the article again. Underline the words and phrases with the same meaning as the words in italics.**

1 Companies who destroy animal habitats should *pay a fine.*

2 You should help to protect animals by *choosing not to buy* fur.

3 We can make it *illegal* to hunt, fish, or trade in endangered species.

4 Governments can *pay for* animal sanctuaries and zoos.

5 If we *work together by taking this action*, we can protect our planet.

CRITICAL THINKING

7 Work with a partner. Discuss the questions.

APPLY

What are some more examples of products that are made from animal parts? Do you use any of these products?

ANALYZE

Should governments spend money to save animal habitats even if this means there is less money for things people need, such as hospitals?

EVALUATE

Why is it a problem if some plants and animals die out?

COLLABORATION

8 **A** Work in a small group. Choose an endangered species and make a fact sheet about it. Include the following information:

- Description of its habitat
- Threats or dangers to it
- Ways to protect it
- Photos of the animal and its habitat

B Present your fact sheets to the class. As a class, choose an endangered species to sponsor.

READING 2

PREPARING TO READ

1 UNDERSTANDING KEY VOCABULARY **Read the definitions. Complete the sentences with the correct form of the words in bold.**

common (adj) happening often or existing in large numbers

cruel (adj) causing pain or suffering on purpose

disease (n) illness; a serious health condition that requires care

fatal (adj) causing death

major (adj) most serious or important

native (adj) used to describe animals and plants that grow naturally in a place

survive (v) to continue to live after almost dying

1 The coyote, a wild member of the dog family, is so ______________ in the western United States that they can be seen in cities.

2 Plastic is often ______________ to sea birds. Millions of birds die each year when they swallow plastic bags and other plastic garbage.

3 The flu is a common ______________ in humans, but some animals, such as horses, birds, seals, and whales, can also get forms of the flu.

4 Many people believe that it is ______________ to keep animals in zoos, where they can't move around freely.

5 Habitat loss is the ______________ cause of species extinction in the Amazon River region.

6 Gray whales are endangered, but there is a chance that they will ______________ because many countries have stopped hunting them.

7 There are many unique species that are ______________ to the island of Madagascar, including more than 80 kinds of snakes.

2 PREDICTING CONTENT USING VISUALS **Work with a partner. Look at the photos in the article on pages 24–25 and discuss the questions.**

1 What are the animals in the photos?

2 Do you have them in your country? How do people feel about them?

3 Which animal do you think is endangered? Why?

LOSING THE BATTLE FOR SURVIVAL

❶ Invasive species

Invasive species are plants and animals that arrive in an area where they are not **native**, usually due to human activity. For example, a species of shellfish might attach itself to the outside of a ship traveling between countries and enter a new environment in this way. Invasive species are often able to grow quickly in their new homes because they have no natural enemies. As a result, they may replace or damage native plants and animals that live in the same environment. One example is the case of gray and red squirrels in Great Britain.

❷ Locations and habitats

Red squirrels used to be a **common** sight in British forests and countryside. Then, in the 1870s, the gray squirrel was introduced from North America because rich people thought the squirrels looked fashionable in the grounds of their large homes. Today, only about 140,000 red squirrels remain, mostly in Scotland. In contrast, gray squirrels are now extremely common and seen as **major** pests due to the damage they cause to plants and houses. While red squirrels are protected, gray squirrels can be legally trapped and destroyed.

❸ Similarities

On first sight, the two species of squirrel are similar. They both have a long tail, which helps them balance when jumping from tree to tree, and the same large eyes, small ears, and powerful back legs.

"TODAY, ONLY ABOUT 140,000 RED SQUIRRELS REMAIN"

Gray squirrel

❹ Differences

In contrast, the two types of squirrel are different in body size and weight. The red squirrel has a typical head-and-body length of approximately 7.5 to 9 inches (19 to 23 centimeters), a tail length of 6 to 8 inches (15 to 20 centimeters) and a body weight of 9 to 12 ounces (250 to 340 grams). The gray squirrel is larger than the red squirrel. The head and body measure between 9 and 12 inches (23 and 30 centimeters), and the tail is between 7.5 and 10 inches (19 and 25 centimeters) long. Adult gray squirrels are also heavier, weighing between 14 and 21 ounces (400 and 600 grams). This size allows them to store more fat and helps them to **survive** hard winters, which could be **fatal** to their smaller cousins.

❺ Why are they endangered?

Three more differences explain why red squirrels have lost out in the competition with gray squirrels. First, red squirrels live high up in the trees, whereas gray squirrels spend more of their time on the ground. This means that any loss of forest habitat greatly affects the red squirrel population. Another reason is that gray squirrels are more intelligent and can adapt to new situations more easily than red squirrels. For example, they can survive in an urban environment because of their ability to use food provided by humans. A third problem for the red squirrel is **disease**. Both squirrels carry the parapox virus. The virus does not seem to affect gray squirrels, but it is fatal to reds.

❻ What can we do?

In conclusion, there does not seem to be much that scientists can do to help red squirrels survive in Great Britain. Some politicians support destroying populations of gray squirrels, but many British people would contend that this is **cruel**. Red squirrels have been successfully reintroduced from other countries, and they could be protected in places where there are no gray squirrels, such as the Isle of Wight. However, some people question whether Britain should protect red squirrels at all. Worldwide, they are not an endangered species. Considering the evidence, saving the red squirrel may be a waste of British government money. Government conservation funding should instead be spent on other endangered animals.

RED SQUIRREL

Length:
7.5in - 9in
Tail length:
6in - 8in
Weight:
9oz - 12oz

GRAY SQUIRREL

Length:
9in - 12in
Tail length:
7.5in - 10in
Weight:
14oz - 21oz

Great Britain

WHILE READING

3 READING FOR MAIN IDEAS **Read the article on pages 24–25 and answer the questions.**

1 What is an invasive species?

____

2 How did the gray squirrel enter Great Britain?

____

3 How are the two species of squirrels similar?

____

4 How are the two species of squirrels different?

____

5 What four reasons are given for the success of the gray squirrel in the U.K.?

____

SKILLS

USING A VENN DIAGRAM

A Venn diagram is useful for taking notes on similarities and differences. It consists of two or three overlapping circles. The Venn diagram in Exercise 4 shows some similarities and differences between red and gray squirrels. The special characteristics of red squirrels are listed on the left side of the diagram. The special characteristics of gray squirrels are on the right. The similarities between red and gray squirrels are listed in the center.

4 TAKING NOTES **Use the Venn diagram to take notes on the similarities and differences between red and gray squirrels.**

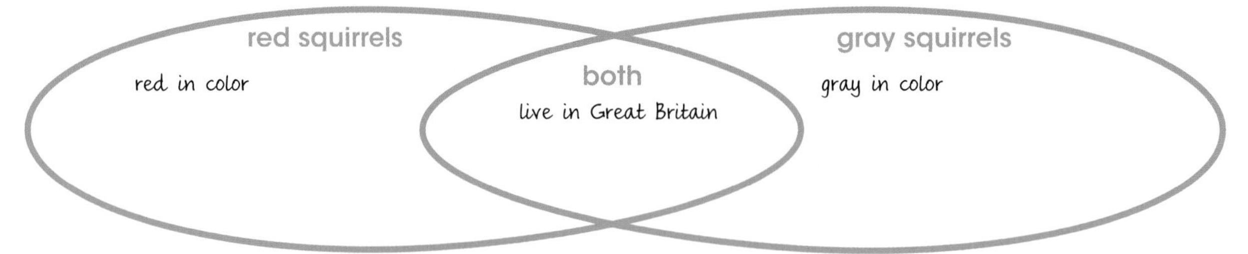

5 SUMMARIZING **Read the summary and circle the correct words to complete it.**

The article uses the example of the red and gray squirrel to explain what can happen when an invasive species competes with a native one. The [1] *gray / red* squirrel was introduced to Britain in the 19th century and has become very successful since then. Now there are [2] *fewer / more than* 140,000 native red squirrels left in the wild. The main reason why the gray squirrel is more successful is that it is [3] *fatter / thinner,* so it is less affected by cold weather. Another reason is that gray squirrels are [4] *unable / able* to live in cities. A further reason may be the parapox virus, which [5] *kills / injures* red squirrels. Even though many people regard the gray squirrel as a [6] *pest / pet,* [7] *most / few* British people support destroying gray squirrels. Because red squirrels [8] *are / aren't* endangered worldwide, perhaps they could be reintroduced to Great Britain.

READING BETWEEN THE LINES

6 MAKING INFERENCES **Read the article again and answer the questions.**

1 Paragraph 1 mentions one way that nonnative species enter a new environment. What are some other ways?

____

2 Why do you think gray squirrels are regarded as "major pests," other than the damage they do to plants and houses?

____

3 What reason could some people give for trying to save the red squirrel?

____

4 Why do you think there are no gray squirrels on the Isle of Wight?

____

CRITICAL THINKING

7 SYNTHESIZING **Work with a partner. Use ideas from Reading 1 and Reading 2 to answer the following questions.**

UNDERSTAND	APPLY	EVALUATE
Which reasons in the readings explain why the red squirrel is an endangered species?	Are introduced animal or plant species a problem in your country? Give examples.	In your opinion, is trying to save endangered species a waste of time and money? Why or why not?

COLLABORATION

8 A Work with a partner. Make a list of five things you can do to help endangered species. Share your list with the class, and add five more things to your list.

B Create a public service announcement (PSA) script about helping endangered species. Find some online examples of PSAs to use as models.

C Record your PSA in audio or video format, and share it with the class.

LANGUAGE DEVELOPMENT

ACADEMIC VERBS

1 Read the sentences. Complete the definitions with the words in bold.

1 Tigers are an endangered species. If people continue to hunt them, it will be impossible for them to **survive**.

2 Very cold and snowy winters **affect** some animals, such as rabbits and squirrels, since they are unable to find food as easily.

3 Seabirds are often hurt due to oil spills. When that happens, biologists catch the birds, clean them, and then **release** them back to nature.

4 If we really want to save endangered species, governments and animal protection organizations need to **cooperate** and stop fighting each other.

5 Sometimes biologists catch endangered animals and **attach** a small radio to their bodies. Then, the biologists always know where the animals are.

6 In this paper, I intend to compare and **contrast** the appearance and behavior of Indian and African elephants.

a ______________ (v) to work together for a particular purpose

b ______________ (v) to influence or cause something to change

c ______________ (v) to allow someone or something to leave a place

d ______________ (v) to stay alive; to continue to exist, especially after an injury or threat

e ______________ (v) to show or explain differences between two people, situations, or things

f ______________ (v) to connect or join one thing to another

COMPARATIVE ADJECTIVES

LANGUAGE

When comparing things, the comparative form of the adjective is used. Use the comparative form of an adjective + *than* to compare two people or things.

Add *-er* to one-syllable adjectives. If the adjective ends in *-e*, just add *-r*.	The red squirrel is **smaller than** the gray squirrel. The gray squirrel is **larger than** the red squirrel.
Use *more/less* + adjective + *than* for adjectives with two or more syllables.	The gray squirrel is **more intelligent than** the red squirrel. The red squirrel is **less common than** the gray squirrel.
If an adjective with two syllables ends in *-y*, remove the *-y* and add *-ier*.	The gray squirrel is **heavier than** the red squirrel.

2 Complete the sentences using the comparative form.

1 The red squirrel is smaller and ______________________ (*weak*) the gray squirrel.

2 Gray squirrels are generally ______________________ (*healthy*) their smaller cousins because grays are not affected by the parapox virus.

3 Gray squirrels are ______________________ (*successful*) red squirrels because they eat food provided by humans.

4 Red squirrels are ______________________ (*endangered*) gray squirrels, which are not at risk of extinction.

WATCH AND LISTEN

GLOSSARY

egret (n) a large white bird with long legs that lives near water

shore (n) the land beside an ocean, a lake, or a river

marsh (n) an area of soft, wet land

depend on (phr v) to need the help of someone or something in order to exist or continue as before

PREPARING TO WATCH

1 ACTIVATING YOUR KNOWLEDGE **You are going to watch a video about dolphins and egrets. Before you watch, work with a partner and discuss the questions.**

1 What do you know about dolphins? Where do they live and what do they eat?

2 What do birds eat? How do they get their food?

2 PREDICTING CONTENT USING VISUALS **Work with a partner. Look at the photos from the video and discuss the questions.**

1 Why and when might dolphins come onto land?

2 Why do you think dolphins live in groups, rather than alone?

3 What is the relationship between the dolphins and the birds?

WHILE WATCHING

3 UNDERSTANDING MAIN IDEAS **Watch the video. Number the sentences in order (1–5).**

a Young dolphins and egrets learn how to fish from their parents. ____

b Dolphins and egrets live together in the marshes of South Carolina. ____

c The dolphins' fishing technique helps the egrets get food. ____

d The egrets watch the dolphins in the water carefully. ____

e The dolphins push the fish onto land. ____

4 UNDERSTANDING DETAILS **Watch the video again. Write *T* (true), *F* (false), or *DNS* (does not say) next to the statements. Then, correct the false statements.**

_____ 1 The egrets are experts on the dolphins' behavior.
_____ 2 The dolphins push the egrets onto the shore.
_____ 3 When the fish are in the water, the dolphins start eating.
_____ 4 The dolphins always use their left sides to push the fish.
_____ 5 Some of the birds do not eat fish.

CRITICAL THINKING

5 **Work with a partner. Discuss the questions.**

APPLY

What animals do humans work with? Why?

ANALYZE

What other animals work together and help each other?

EVALUATE

Why would two different animals work together?

COLLABORATION

6 **A** Work in a small group. Record a 30-second video of birds, fish, insects, or animals outside of class on your phone. Answer the questions about your video subject.

- Where does it live?
- What does it eat?
- What is its most dangerous threat?
- What kind of relationship does it have with humans?
- Should we protect it? Why or why not?

B Prepare a script for your video. Include an introduction, answers to the questions, and a conclusion. Show your video clip and read your script to the class.

UNIT 2

THE ENVIRONMENT

LEARNING OBJECTIVES

Key Reading Skills	Reading for details; taking notes on causes and effects
Additional Reading Skills	Understanding key vocabulary; predicting content using visuals; reading for main ideas; scanning to find information; identifying purpose; previewing; summarizing; making inferences; synthesizing
Language Development	Academic vocabulary; environment collocations

ACTIVATE YOUR KNOWLEDGE

Work with a partner. Discuss the questions.

1 Is the weather changing in your country? How?

2 What are some ways that humans have affected the environment?

3 What is the biggest environmental problem in your country?

READING 1

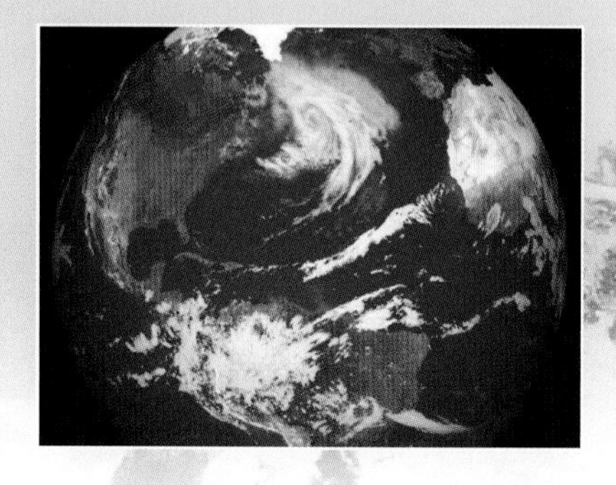

PREPARING TO READ

1 UNDERSTANDING KEY VOCABULARY **You are going to read a Web page about climate change. Before you do, read the sentences below. Complete the definitions with the words in bold.**

1 The Amazon rainforest is one of the largest **ecosystems** in the world. It is home to more than 10% of all the known plants and animals on Earth.

2 Southern California has a very pleasant **climate**. The winters are not too cold and the summers are not too hot.

3 Pesticides—chemicals generally used to kill insects that damage plants—also **threaten** helpful insects, such as bees.

4 In order to fight pollution, scientists are developing car engines that use electric or solar energy instead of **fossil fuels** like gasoline.

5 Methane (CH^4) is a **greenhouse gas** that is found naturally inside the Earth and under the sea. It is used for cooking and heating homes and buildings.

6 The Earth's **atmosphere** is 300 miles (480 km) thick and contains a mixture of about 10 different gases, which we call *air*.

7 Because of **global warming**, polar ice is melting, sea levels are rising, and some islands might soon be underwater.

8 Habitat loss is the most important **cause** of species extinction.

a ______________ (n) a gas that makes the air around the Earth warmer

b ______________ (n) someone or something that makes something happen

c ______________ (n) the layer of gases around the Earth

d ______________ (n) the general weather conditions usually found in a particular place

e ______________ (n) an increase in the Earth's temperature because of pollution

f ______________ (v) to be likely to damage or harm something

g ______________ (n) all the living things in an area and the effect they have on each other and the environment

h ______________ (n) a source of energy like coal, gas, and petroleum, that was formed inside the Earth millions of years ago

2 PREDICTING CONTENT USING VISUALS **Work with a partner. Look at the photo of the Upsala glacier on pages 36–37 and discuss the questions.**

1. What do you think has happened to the glacier?
2. What do you think caused this transformation?
3. What are some other places where a similar transformation is happening today?
4. How do you think this will affect the world?

Our Changing Planet

The Upsala glacier in Argentina used to be one of the biggest glaciers in South America. In 1928, it was covered in ice and snow, but now the glacier is melting at an annual rate of about 650 feet (about 200 meters), so the area is covered in water. This is evidence of global warming.

Effects of Climate Change

1 In the last 100 years, the global temperature has gone up by around 1.33°F (0.75°C). This may not sound like much, but such a small increase is causing sea levels to rise and **threatening** the habitat of many species of plants and animals. An increase of 3.6°F (2°C) in global temperatures could result in extinction for 30% of the world's land species.

2 The Northwest Passage is a sea route that runs along the northern coast of Canada between the Atlantic and the Pacific Oceans. In the past, it was often difficult to use because the water was frozen; however, increasing temperatures and the subsequent deglaciation[1] have made it easier for ships to travel through this route. The trouble is that the melting of the ice will lead to loss of habitat for the polar bears and other species that live in this area.

3 Experts predict that global sea levels could rise by 12 to 48 inches (30.5 to 122 centimeters) by the end of the century. Consequently, some areas that were land a few hundred years ago are now underwater, and many low-lying islands may be underwater in the future.

4 As a result of the changing **climate**, the world's **ecosystems** are also changing faster than ever before. More than one-third of the world's mangrove forests[2] and around 20% of the world's coral reefs[3] have been destroyed in the last few decades. Forests are being cut down to provide land for food, because human population is growing at such a rapid rate. Approximately a quarter of the land on Earth is now used for growing food. As a result of the higher temperatures and higher levels of carbon dioxide in the **atmosphere**, plants are producing more pollen, which could lead to more cases of asthma, a medical condition that makes it hard to breathe.

Causes of Climate Change

5 What is causing climate change? The main **cause** is the huge amount of **greenhouse gases**, such as methane and carbon dioxide (CO_2), in the atmosphere, but the reason for the high levels is the world's population—you and I. As the population increases, more land is needed to provide food and energy. Burning **fossil fuels** for heating, lighting, transportation, electricity, or manufacturing produces CO_2. Furthermore, humans breathe out CO_2 while trees "breathe in" CO_2 and produce oxygen, so by cutting down trees, we are increasing the amount of CO_2 in the atmosphere and reducing the amount of oxygen. As a result of human activities, CO_2 levels are now at their highest in 800,000 years.

What Can Be Done

6 The biggest challenge we all face is to prevent further environmental disasters. We must do something before it is too late. We need to reduce the amount of CO_2 in the atmosphere. We need to stop burning fossil fuels and start using renewable energy. We can get enough energy from renewable fuels such as solar energy, hydroelectric energy, or wind power to be able to stop using fossil fuels completely.

Click here to sign the petition to tell governments to take action before it is too late!

[1] **deglaciation** (n) the melting of a glacier
[2] **mangrove forests** (n) large areas of trees and shrubs that live in coastal areas, e.g., in Florida and Bangladesh
[3] **coral reefs** (n) diverse underwater ecosystems built by tiny animals

WHILE READING

3 READING FOR MAIN IDEAS **Read the Web page, and number the main ideas in the order that they are mentioned.**

solution to the problem ______

changing ecosystems ______

melting glaciers ______

causes of climate change ______

4 SCANNING TO FIND INFORMATION **Read the Web page again. Complete the sentences using the words and phrases in the box.**

CO_2 levels	coral reefs	extinction	farming
global sea levels	global temperatures	mangrove forests	

1 Over the last century, ______________ have gone up by 0.75 degrees Celsius.

2 Global increases in temperature could cause the ______________ of 30% of land species.

3 ______________ could rise by about 12 inches by the end of the century.

4 Recently, over a third of the world's ______________ have been destroyed.

5 Twenty percent of the Earth's ______________ have been lost in the last few decades.

6 Twenty-five percent of the land on Earth is used for ______________.

7 ______________ are at their highest for 800,000 years.

SKILLS

READING FOR DETAILS

In a paragraph, the sentences that come after the topic sentence contain *supporting details*—information to help the reader understand the main idea more fully. Types of supporting details include facts, statistics, examples, reasons, explanations, comparisons, and descriptions.

Often, the topic sentence includes words that tell you what type of supporting sentences to expect in the body of the paragraph. For example:

Topic sentence: What is causing climate change?

The words *is causing* tell you that the paragraph will use causes, or reasons, to explain the main idea.

5 READING FOR DETAILS **Read the Web page again and complete the chart with supporting details.**

1 country where the Upsala glacier is located	
2 name of sea route through the Arctic ice	
3 why forests are being cut down all over the world	
4 medical problem caused by pollen	
5 main chemicals responsible for climate change	
6 human activities that reduce the amount of oxygen in the atmosphere	
7 how to reduce the amount of CO_2 in the atmosphere	

READING BETWEEN THE LINES

6 IDENTIFYING PURPOSE **Why did the author write the Web page? Circle the correct answer.**

a To inform the reader about the causes of melting glaciers

b To educate the reader about how to stop climate change

c To convince people to sign a petition about using renewable fuels

CRITICAL THINKING

7 Work with a partner. Discuss the questions.

REMEMBER

What is the advantage to the melting of the glaciers in the Northwest Passage?

ANALYZE

What are the possible disadvantages of using renewable energy like solar or wind?

EVALUATE

Why don't governments, corporations, and individuals do more to help prevent global warming?

COLLABORATION

8 **A** Work in a small group. Make a list of ten things you, the government, and/or corporations can do to reduce global warming and slow climate change. Discuss and put them in order of importance.

B Present your best ideas to the class. Each person should discuss one idea.

READING 2

PREPARING TO READ

1 UNDERSTANDING KEY VOCABULARY **Read the definitions. Complete the sentences with the correct form of the words in bold.**

absorb (v) to take in a liquid or gas through a surface and hold it

construction (n) the process of building something, usually large structures such as houses, roads, or bridges

destruction (n) the act of causing so much damage to something that it stops existing because it cannot be repaired

effect (n) result; a change that happens because of a cause

farming (n) the job of working on a farm or organizing work on a farm

logging (n) the activity or business of cutting down trees for wood

rainforest (n) a forest in a tropical area that gets a lot of rain

1 Clothes made from plants, like cotton or bamboo, ______________ water more easily than man-made materials like polyester.

2 ______________ has been the occupation of my family since my grandfather bought his first cow 75 years ago.

3 ______________ hurts native people because it destroys the forest that provides them with food, shelter, and medicine.

4 The Amazon ______________ in South America receives 60 to 118 inches (150 to 300 centimeters) of rain every year.

5 Because of heavy snow, the ______________ of the new road stopped for more than two months.

6 Sunburn is just one of the harmful ______________ of too much sun on sensitive skin.

7 Hurricane Katrina in 2005 caused serious ______________ along the U.S. coast from Florida to Texas and killed more than 1,800 people.

2 PREVIEWING **You are going to read an academic article about deforestation. Before you read, look at the title and photos on pages 42–43. Then answer the questions.**

1 Why are trees important for the environment?

____

____

2 Why do people cut down trees?

____

____

3 What will happen if we destroy too many trees?

____

____

The Dangers of Deforestation

1 Forests, which cover almost one-third of the surface of the Earth, produce oxygen and provide homes to plants, animals, and humans. These days, many of the world's great forests are threatened by deforestation: the process of removing trees from large areas of land. The **destruction** of forests occurs for several reasons: trees are used as fuel or for **construction**, and cleared land is used as pasture[1] for animals and fields for planting food. The main harmful **effects** of deforestation are climate change and damage to animal habitats.

2 The main causes of deforestation are commercial **farming** by big business and farming by local people. Huge commercial farms have taken over large areas of forest in many countries. In Indonesia, for example, industrial **logging** is carried out to clear huge areas for the production of palm oil, while in Brazil, large areas of the Amazon **rainforest** are cleared to grow soy and vegetable oil. In contrast, local farmers may cut down and burn trees to clear an area just big enough to graze cattle or grow crops. However, after two or three years, the land can no longer be used, so the farmer moves to another piece of land. Normally, it takes around ten years for cleared land to recover, but in populated areas, the land is never allowed to recover. This constant reuse of land leads to heavy erosion—the loss of the top layer of soil that protects the ground. Erosion, in turn, can cause flooding in heavy rain.

[1]**pasture** (n) an area of land with grass for animals to eat
[2]**biodiversity** (n) the variety of different animals and plants in an area

3 One serious effect of deforestation is climate change. Normally tropical rainforests help control the Earth's temperature by absorbing carbon dioxide. As an example, the vast rainforest of the Amazon covers an area of more than 2.6 million square miles—about 10 times the size of Texas—and **absorbs** an estimated 1.5 billion tons of carbon dioxide annually. However, in areas where deforestation has taken place, the carbon dioxide goes into the atmosphere and traps heat in a process called the greenhouse effect. The result is global warming. Increasing global temperatures result in less rain. This causes the rainforests to dry out and leads to fires—which cause more emissions of carbon dioxide. In this way, the rainforests actually contribute to global warming instead of helping to solve it.

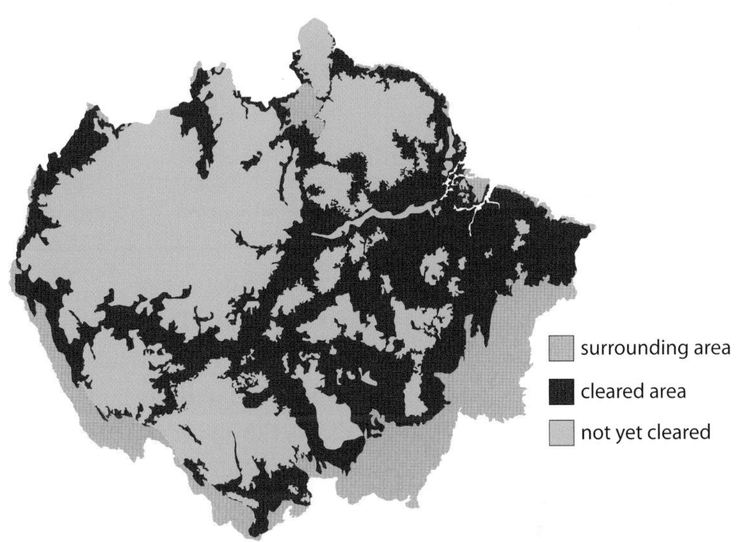

Large areas of the Amazon rainforest have been destroyed.

4 Forest destruction also has an effect on biodiversity[2]. Deforestation causes the loss of habitats and damage to land where plants and animal species live, leading to the extinction of many species. A decrease in biodiversity threatens entire ecosystems and destroys future sources of food and medicine.

5 In conclusion, damage to the world's forests is leading to changes in the natural environment and causing global warming. Looking to the future, governments should act to plant more trees that will absorb carbon dioxide and protect forests from illegal logging. Otherwise, deforestation on such a large scale is sure to have terrible effects on the environment.

“Increasing global temperatures lead to forest fires.”

WHILE READING

3 SUMMARIZING **Read the article. Complete the summary with the words in the box.**

animals	crops	decade	deforestation	effects
environment	erosion	habitats	protected	warming

The article discusses the human causes of (1)____________________ and the (2)____________ on the environment. Trees are removed for grazing of (3)____________ and growing (4)____________ like soy and palm oil. Farmers traditionally leave the land for a (5)____________ before reusing it, but if the land is constantly reused, it results in (6)____________ of the soil. Deforestation allows CO_2 to escape into the atmosphere and contributes to global (7)____________. It also affects biodiversity because it leads to the loss of (8)____________. Governments should make sure forests are (9)____________ from logging. Otherwise, deforestation will have terrible consequences for the (10)____________.

4 READING FOR DETAILS **Read the article again. Correct the mistakes in the sentences.**

1 In Indonesia, trees are cut down to make way for olive oil plantations.
2 Farmers can graze animals on their land for ten years.
3 The rainforests of the Amazon cover an area 10 times the size of the U.S.
4 Deforestation protects future sources of food and medicine.
5 Governments should plant more trees to absorb oxygen.
6 Small-scale deforestation will have disastrous effects on the environment.

SKILLS

TAKING NOTES ON CAUSES AND EFFECTS

Look for causes and effects when you read academic texts. Sometimes they are discussed in separate paragraphs. For example:

Problem: traffic congestion in my city

Cause: too many cars on the road

Effects: air pollution; noise; people are often late to work or school; accidents

Sometimes they are connected in a chain of events in the same paragraph. For example:

Cause 1: a shortage of housing → **Effect 1:** people live in the suburbs →

Cause 2: people live in the suburbs → **Effect 2:** they must drive to get to work

Use a chart to take notes on causes and effects.

5 TAKING NOTES **Work in a small group. Look back at the article. Underline three causes of deforestation and circle three effects. Then complete the chart.**

DEFORESTATION

CAUSES		EFFECTS
commercial farming by big business	→	

READING BETWEEN THE LINES

6 MAKING INFERENCES **Work with a partner. Discuss the questions.**

1 What does the writer mean by the phrases *industrial logging* and *commercial farming*?

2 What will probably happen if the Amazon rainforest disappears?

3 Why does deforestation reduce future sources of food and medicine?

CRITICAL THINKING

7 SYNTHESIZING **Work with a partner. Use information from Reading 1 and Reading 2 to answer the questions.**

UNDERSTAND

As the world's climate changes, which places will have too much water? Which places will become drier?

EVALUATE

How do both the melting of the glaciers and deforestation contribute to the extinction of species?

COLLABORATION

8 **A** Work with a partner. Look online for organizations that work to stop deforestation or slow climate change. Choose one, and research their work. Answer these questions:

- What is their mission, or goal?
- Where do they get money for their work?
- What is one of their successful projects or programs?

B Report your findings to the class. As a class, vote on the organization that is making the biggest difference.

LANGUAGE DEVELOPMENT

ACADEMIC VOCABULARY

1 Replace the underlined words in the sentences with the academic words in the box.

annual (adj)	areas (n)	challenge (n)	consequences (n)
contributes to (v)	issue (n)	predict (v)	trend (n)

1 The most serious problem that threatens the environment is climate change. ______________

2 Experts think that there will not be enough fresh water in the future.

____

3 Pollution and climate change are the effects of human activity. ______________

4 Fortunately, we are seeing a pattern where people recycle more and use less packaging. ______________

5 In some places, the glaciers have melted or even disappeared as a result of higher temperatures. ______________

6 The yearly rate of species loss in the rainforest is nearly 50,000—that's 135 plant, animal, and insect species each day! ______________

7 The biggest test we face is to protect the planet. ______________

8 Human activity causes climate change. ______________

ENVIRONMENT COLLOCATIONS

2 Match the nouns to make collocations about the environment.

1	climate	a	group
2	environmental	b	plant
3	tropical	c	change
4	carbon	d	gas
5	power	e	rainforest
6	natural	f	resource
7	greenhouse	g	dioxide

3 Complete the sentences with the correct form of the collocations from Exercise 2.

1. In my town, about 70% of the electricity comes from a ______________________ that uses coal for energy.
2. Carbon dioxide and methane are examples of ______________________.
3. Almost all scientists these days agree that ______________________ is happening and it is a serious threat to our planet.
4. Trees absorb ______________________ and give off oxygen.
5. All over the world, ______________________ are working to educate people about the dangers of deforestation and habitat destruction.
6. Fresh water is the most precious ______________________ on Earth.
7. Thousands of unique plants, animals, birds, and insects live in the ______________________ of South America and Southeast Asia.

WATCH AND LISTEN

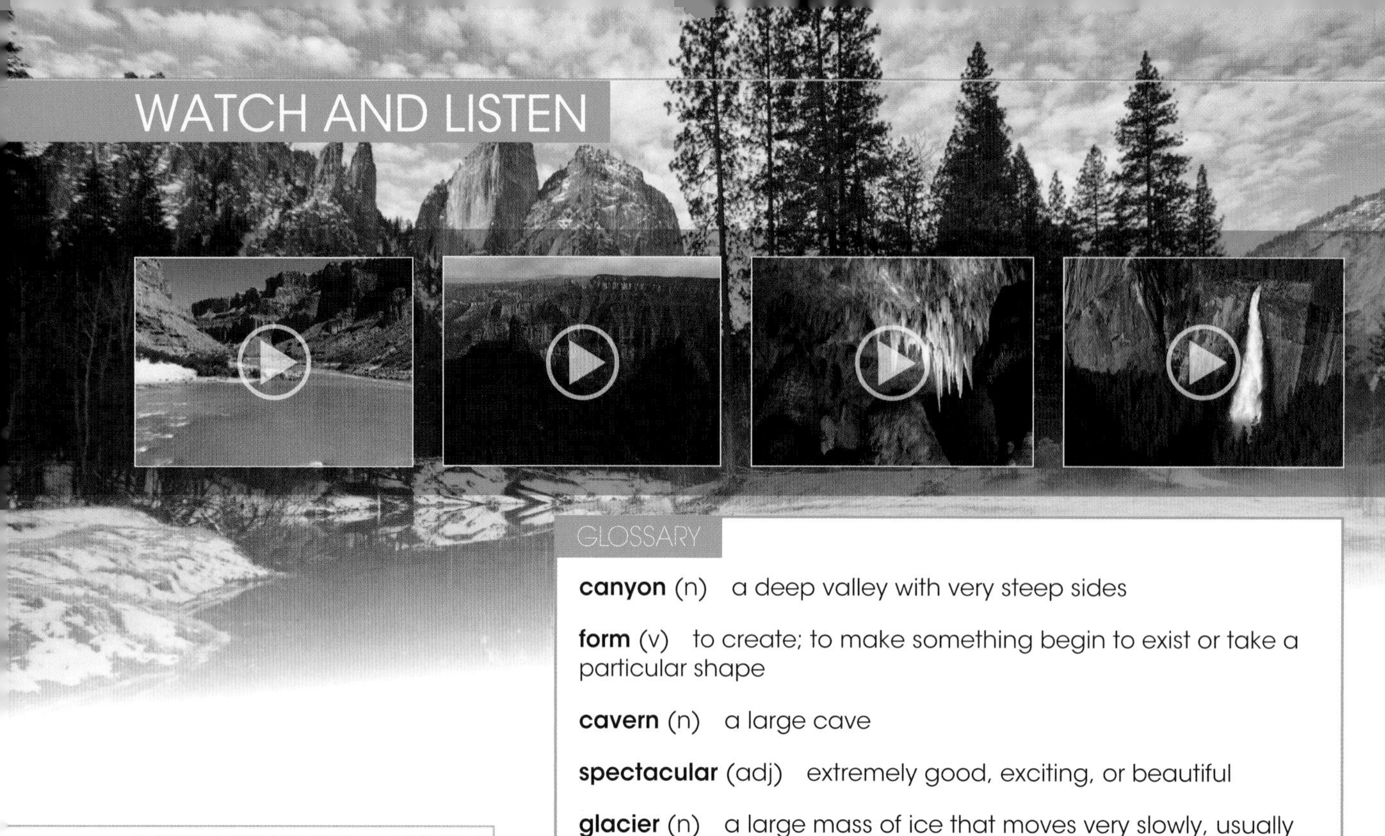

GLOSSARY

canyon (n) a deep valley with very steep sides

form (v) to create; to make something begin to exist or take a particular shape

cavern (n) a large cave

spectacular (adj) extremely good, exciting, or beautiful

glacier (n) a large mass of ice that moves very slowly, usually down a slope or valley

PREPARING TO WATCH

1 ACTIVATING YOUR KNOWLEDGE **You are going to watch a video about the natural environment. Before you watch, work with a partner and discuss the questions.**

1 What are the Seven Natural Wonders of the World?
2 What are some important geographical features, like mountains or rivers, in your country?
3 What street or place names in your city or country refer to geography? (e.g., Pacific Coast Highway, Lake Street)

2 PREDICTING CONTENT USING VISUALS **Work with a partner. Look at the photos from the video and discuss the questions.**

1 Where are these places located?
2 How old do you think these places are?
3 Who owns these places?

WHILE WATCHING

3 UNDERSTANDING MAIN IDEAS **Watch the video. Number the sentences in order (1–6).**

_____ a The weather in the Grand Canyon can change very quickly.
_____ b Water is still changing the inside of Carlsbad Caverns.
_____ c Half Dome in Yosemite National Park was made by glaciers.
_____ d The Colorado River formed the Grand Canyon.
_____ e The rocks in the Grand Canyon are very old.
_____ f Yosemite Falls is the tallest waterfall in North America.

4 UNDERSTANDING DETAILS **Watch the video again. Circle the correct answer.**

1 The Grand Canyon was formed in ______ years.
 a a million
 b a few million
 c a billion

2 Some of the rocks in the Grand Canyon are ______ the Earth.
 a as old as
 b half as old as
 c almost as old as

3 The weather in the Grand Canyon can suddenly change from ______.
 a hot to dry
 b dry to wet
 c hot to cold

4 The Carlsbad Caverns is the ______ cave system in North America.
 a oldest
 b largest
 c widest

5 The water in Yosemite National Park comes from ______.
 a snow
 b glaciers
 c a cave

CRITICAL THINKING

5 **Work with a partner. Discuss the questions.**

APPLY

What other natural wonders were created by water?

ANALYZE

How might water change the Earth's geography in the next 100 years?

EVALUATE

In your opinion, who should protect special natural areas in the world?

COLLABORATION

6 **A** Work in a small group. Choose one of the Seven Natural Wonders of the World. Research the place and prepare a presentation for your class. Answer these questions:

- Where is the natural wonder?
- Why is it special?
- What is its history?
- Is it affected by climate change? How?
- Are there any other threats to it?
- How is it protected?

B Present your natural wonder to the class. Answer questions.

UNIT 3

TRANSPORTATION

LEARNING OBJECTIVES	
Key Reading Skill	Predicting content using visuals
Additional Reading Skills	Understanding key vocabulary; reading for main ideas; reading for details; making inferences; taking notes; synthesizing
Language Development	Transportation collocations; synonyms for verbs

ACTIVATE YOUR KNOWLEDGE

1 Work with a partner. Look at the photo. How many different types of transportation can you name?

2 Which modes of transportation do you usually use?

3 Why do you use these modes of transportation?

4 Why do you not use the other modes of transportation?

READING 1

PREPARING TO READ

1 UNDERSTANDING KEY VOCABULARY **Read the definitions. Complete the sentences with the correct form of the words in bold.**

commuter (n) someone who travels between home and work or school regularly

connect (v) to join two things or places together

destination (n) the place where someone or something is going

outskirts (n) the outer area of a city or town

public transportation (n) a system of vehicles, such as buses and subways, which operate at regular times for public use

rail (n) trains as a method of transportation

traffic congestion (n) when too many vehicles use a road network and it results in slower speeds or no movement at all

1 Vancouver, British Columbia, has an outstanding system of ________________, so it isn't necessary to own a car there.

2 I like living on the ________________ of the city because there is more open space and the air is cleaner.

3 I take the train to work every day because the ________________ network is fast and cheap.

4 ________________ has improved since my city built a subway and improved the bus system. Fewer people drive to work now.

5 I told the bus driver that my ________________ was downtown, so she told me to get off on Main Street.

6 In large cities, people usually prefer to live near their workplace so that they don't have to be a ________________, but it's more expensive than the suburbs.

7 Ferries ________________ the mainland to the islands.

SKILLS

PREDICTING CONTENT USING VISUALS

The images that accompany a text can provide valuable information about the content. For example, they can tell you where the text is set, what it is about, what kind of text it is (essay, blog post, etc.), what the key points are, and much more. All this information helps you make predictions about what you are going to read, and once you start reading, it helps you focus on the important information in the reading.

2 PREDICTING CONTENT USING VISUALS **Work with a partner. You are going to read a case study about a new kind of city. Before you read, look at the photos of transportation on this page and on pages 54–55 and answer the questions.**

1 What problem can you see in the photo on this page? Does your city have this problem?

____

2 What do you think the vehicle is in the top photo on page 55? How could it be a solution to the problem in Question 1? Where do you think the photo was taken?

____

____

3 What other solutions do you think the case study will discuss?

____

CASE STUDY

Masdar: the Future of Cities?

A Modern Problem

1 Abu Dhabi, the capital of the United Arab Emirates, is a modern city with a population of about 1.5 million people. The expanding economy and rising population have brought great benefits to Abu Dhabi, but with them comes a major problem: traffic jams. Abu Dhabi, like many cities in the United Arab Emirates, suffers from **traffic congestion**, and although it is not as bad as in some cities, the average commuting time of 45 minutes is relatively high.

solar panel

A Unique Solution

2 One answer to the congestion problem is Masdar City, a new city of 2.3 square miles (6 square kilometers) being built near the airport on the **outskirts** of Abu Dhabi. Masdar gets all of its electricity from solar power. There is a wall around the city to keep out the hot desert wind, and the streets are narrow. This provides shade from the sun and allows a breeze to pass through the streets. As a result, the city can feel up to 70 °F (21 °C) cooler than Abu Dhabi feels.

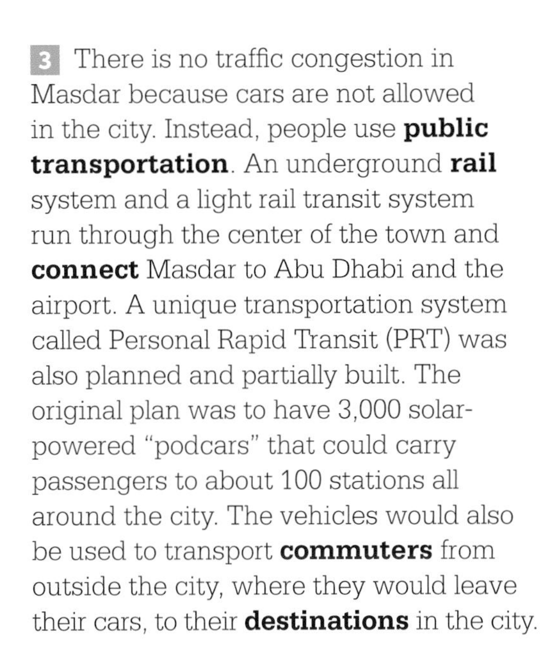

3 There is no traffic congestion in Masdar because cars are not allowed in the city. Instead, people use **public transportation**. An underground **rail** system and a light rail transit system run through the center of the town and **connect** Masdar to Abu Dhabi and the airport. A unique transportation system called Personal Rapid Transit (PRT) was also planned and partially built. The original plan was to have 3,000 solar-powered "podcars" that could carry passengers to about 100 stations all around the city. The vehicles would also be used to transport **commuters** from outside the city, where they would leave their cars, to their **destinations** in the city.

Personal Rapid Transit podcar

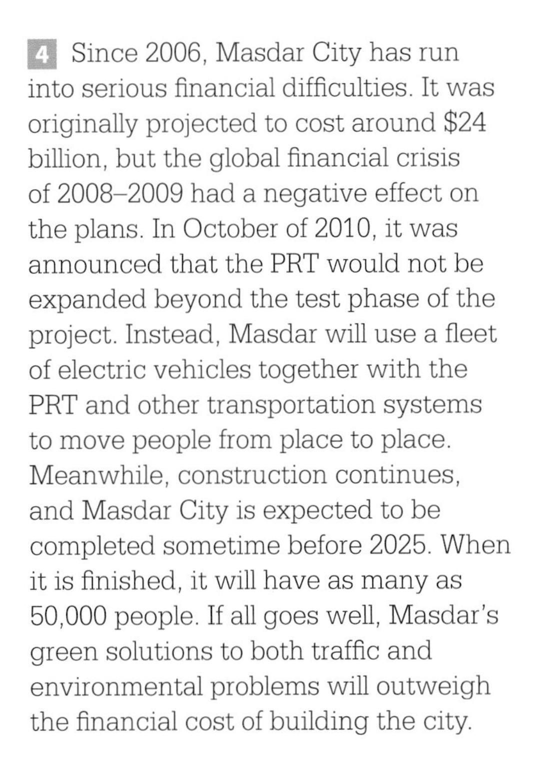

4 Since 2006, Masdar City has run into serious financial difficulties. It was originally projected to cost around $24 billion, but the global financial crisis of 2008–2009 had a negative effect on the plans. In October of 2010, it was announced that the PRT would not be expanded beyond the test phase of the project. Instead, Masdar will use a fleet of electric vehicles together with the PRT and other transportation systems to move people from place to place. Meanwhile, construction continues, and Masdar City is expected to be completed sometime before 2025. When it is finished, it will have as many as 50,000 people. If all goes well, Masdar's green solutions to both traffic and environmental problems will outweigh the financial cost of building the city.

Masdar City

WHILE READING

3 **Read the case study on pages 54–55. Then look back at your answers to Exercise 2 on page 53. Would you answer any of the questions differently now?**

4 READING FOR MAIN IDEAS **Read the case study again and answer the questions.**

1 Which features are designed to make Masdar City cooler than the area around it?

____

____

2 What is a PRT, and how does it work?

____

____

3 Apart from the PRT, what other transportation options are available in Masdar City?

____

____

4 How did the financial crisis of 2008–2009 affect Masdar City?

____

____

5 READING FOR DETAILS **Read the case study again. Complete each sentence with no more than two words.**

1 Abu Dhabi has a big problem with ______________ .
2 The average time it takes to get to work is ______________ .
3 Masdar's electricity comes from ______________ .
4 Traffic jams are not a problem in Masdar because cars are ______________ in the city.
5 Originally, Masdar City was supposed to cost $ ______________ .
6 Masdar City will be completed by ______________ , and ______________ people will live there.

READING BETWEEN THE LINES

6 MAKING INFERENCES **Work with a partner. Read the case study again and answer the questions.**

1 What are the possible benefi ts of Abu Dhabi's expanding economy and rising population?

____

____

2 Masdar will be a small city with several advantages. What will be some disadvantages of living there?

____

____

3 Why do you think the planners of Masdar City decided to stop building the PRT?

____

____

CRITICAL THINKING

7 **Work with a partner. Discuss the questions.**

APPLY

Would you like to live in Masdar City? Why or why not?

APPLY

Do you agree that the benefits of Masdar City will outweigh the financial cost of building it? Why or why not?

EVALUATE

Would a PRT system work in your city? Why or why not?

COLLABORATION

8 **A** Work with a partner. Brainstorm a list of at least 10 problems that modern cities have. Then list a possible future solution for each problem, for example:

Problem	Solution
pollution	electric cars

B Create a survey with five of the problems and solutions in your list. Ask your classmates to rate your solutions from 1 (best) to 5 (worst). Then compare the top ideas from each survey.

READING 2

PREPARING TO READ

1 UNDERSTANDING KEY VOCABULARY **Read the definitions. Complete the sentences with the correct form of the words in bold.**

cycle (v) to travel by bicycle

emergency (n) an unexpected situation that requires immediate action

engineering (n) the activity of designing and building things like bridges, roads, machines, etc.

fuel (n) a substance like gas or coal that produces energy when it is burned

government (n) the group of people that controls a country or city and makes decisions about laws, taxes, education, etc.

practical (adj) useful; suitable for the situation it is being used for

vehicle (n) any machine that travels on roads, such as cars, buses, etc.

1 I don't own a car, but I have a bicycle. I usually ____________ to work if the weather is nice.

2 In my apartment I have a first-aid kit, a fire extinguisher, and a flashlight in case of an ____________ .

3 The Danyang-Kunshan Grand Bridge in China, which is 103 miles (166 km) long, is an incredible work of ____________ .

4 A Boeing 747 jet burns about 11 tons of ______________ an hour in flight. That's equal to about 1 gallon (3.8 liters) each second.

5 The ______________ wants people to drive less, so it passed a law that requires drivers to pay a high tax on gas.

6 In Masdar, drivers must park their ______________ outside the city and use public transportation to reach the city center.

7 If I want to use public transportation, I must take three buses to get to school. This isn't ______________, so I usually drive my car.

2 PREDICTING CONTENT USING VISUALS **Work with a partner. You are going to read an essay about solving traffic congestion. Before you read, look at the photos on pages 60–61 and answer the questions.**

1 What solutions to the problem of traffic congestion do the photographs show?

____

____

2 What other solutions to traffic congestion do you think the article will discuss?

____

____

How Big Is the Problem?

1 Traffic congestion is a serious problem in cities worldwide. There are simply too many **vehicles** competing for too little space. The company TomTom, which does research on traffic in cities worldwide, estimated that in 2015, the average commuter wasted 100 hours during the evening rush hour alone. In addition to wasting people's time, traffic jams have many other negative effects. Therefore, **governments** everywhere are working hard to find solutions to this problem.

2 Traffic jams have negative effects on drivers, cities, and the environment. To begin, they cause stress to drivers, which may lead to health problems or road rage[1]. Traffic jams can also lead to economic losses because products cannot be delivered on time, and employees arrive late for work or meetings. Another negative effect is that **emergency** services can become caught in traffic and are therefore unable to get to an emergency in time. Finally, traffic congestion negatively affects the environment. Traffic congestion wastes **fuel**, which in turn produces more carbon dioxide through car exhaust[2] and contributes to the greenhouse effect. Taken together, all these effects have a serious negative impact on the quality of people's lives.

What Can Be Done?

3 Because of these serious effects, cities and governments everywhere are taking steps to reduce road congestion. The most obvious solutions involve **engineering**. This means building more roads with wider lanes so that more cars can travel at the same time. Also, tunnels and bridges can be constructed to guide drivers around congested areas. However, the construction costs for engineering solutions are extremely high. Another problem is that more roads may actually result in more traffic. In short, engineering solutions have both advantages and disadvantages.

4 Other, more creative, solutions to the congestion problem are to increase the tax on fuel or to make people pay to travel in the center of a city or on a freeway. If governments increase the cost of driving, people will think more carefully about using their cars. However, taxing fuel and roads may mean that some people cannot afford to drive their cars, and they may have to give up their jobs. Also, governments may not want to increase the fuel tax too much if the tax is unpopular with voters.

5 A more popular solution, therefore, would be to promote other forms of transportation, like ferries, and subways. One suggestion is to encourage people to **cycle** more. Although riding a bicycle has obvious health benefits and does not pollute the air, it is not **practical** in every climate and can prove dangerous in heavy traffic.

6 Another possibility is to persuade people to use buses, although they are inconvenient for some people. A related option is a park-and-ride system that allows people to drive to the outskirts of cities, park, and then take a bus to the city center. This allows some flexibility for car drivers and reduces congestion in the center of the city. A disadvantage for people who work late shifts[3] is that many buses do not run at night.

7 Overall, cities are using a variety of methods to tackle the problem of traffic congestion. Most of the methods have advantages as well as disadvantages. It seems that encouraging alternative forms of transportation is probably the best solution because it reduces the amount of traffic on the roads and also has a positive effect on the environment.

[1] **road rage** (n) violence committed by angry drivers in traffic
[2] **exhaust** (n) smoke that comes out of a car as a result of burning gasoline
[3] **late shifts** (n) work hours that are late in the day or at night

WHILE READING

3 READING FOR MAIN IDEAS **Read the essay on pages 60–61 and circle the best title.**

a The Effects of Traffic Congestion in Cities
b Solving the Problem of Traffic Congestion
c Urban Traffic Congestion is Increasing
d Bicycles Can Solve Urban Traffic Congestion

4 READING FOR DETAILS **Read the essay again. What are the four negative effects of traffic congestion mentioned in the essay? Write your answers.**

____

____

____

____

5 TAKING NOTES **Read the essay again. Complete the chart of solutions to the problem of traffic congestion.**

solutions	advantages	disadvantages
Engineering: Build more roads, tunnels, and bridges.		
Tax: Increase tax on roads and fuel.		
Cycling: Encourage people to cycle more.		
Park-and-ride: People park and then travel into the city center by bicycle.		

READING BETWEEN THE LINES

6 MAKING INFERENCES **Work with a partner. Answer the questions.**

1 What sort of health problems might be caused by stress?

____

____

2 Why would a person in the government not want to have an unpopular tax?

____

____

3 Why are buses inconvenient for some people?

____

____

CRITICAL THINKING

7 SYNTHESIZING **Work with a partner. Use ideas from Reading 1 and Reading 2 to discuss the questions.**

APPLY

Are Abu Dhabi's traffic poblems similar to the problems in other big cities? Give an example.

EVALUATE

Look at the chart in Exercise 5 on page 62. Which solution do you think is the best? Why?

CREATE

In addition to the solutions suggested in the readings, can you develop other solutions to traffic congestion?

COLLABORATION

8 **A** Work in a small group. Research a city that is using new solutions to their traffic problems, such as public bicycles or apps that monitor traffic in real time. Consider these questions:

- How is the solution new or different?
- How successful is it?
- What are some advantages and disadvantages?
- How is the city working on the disadvantages?
- What do you think of the solution?

B Give a group presentation to the class. Get feedback and discuss which solutions might be good ideas for other cities.

LANGUAGE DEVELOPMENT

TRANSPORTATION COLLOCATIONS

1 Match the words to make collocations about transportation.

1	traffic	a	transportation
2	public	b	restrictions
3	bike	c	congestion
4	rush	d	lane
5	car	e	pool
6	road	f	rage
7	parking	g	hour

2 Complete the sentences with collocations from Exercise 1.

1 ______________ is a big problem in this city. The traffic jams are terrible.

2 I use ______________ like trains or the subway to get to work.

3 You can't drive in the ______________. It's only for bicycles.

4 Because of ______________, you can't leave your car there.

5 ______________ is usually from eight to nine in the morning, and then again from four in the afternoon to seven in the evening

6 I am in a ______________ and drive to work with a coworker.

7 If people get angry and behave aggressively in traffic, they are expressing ______________.

SYNONYMS FOR VERBS

3 Rewrite the sentences using the verbs from the box to replace the words in bold.

attempt	consider	convince	prevent
produce	reduce	require	waste

1 We **need** more public transportation in the city like a light-rail network.

____

2 Commuters **try** to arrive on time, but traffic often causes delays.

____

3 Masdar City is going to use solar energy to **make** all of its electricity.

____

4 It's important for people in industrial countries to **lower** their use of energy.

____

5 Traffic congestion causes people to **use** time and energy **in an inefficient way**.

____

6 We should **think about** cycling instead of using our cars to travel short distances.

____

7 New roads will **stop** traffic congestion in the short term.

____

8 It will be difficult to **get** drivers to use public transportation.

____

WATCH AND LISTEN

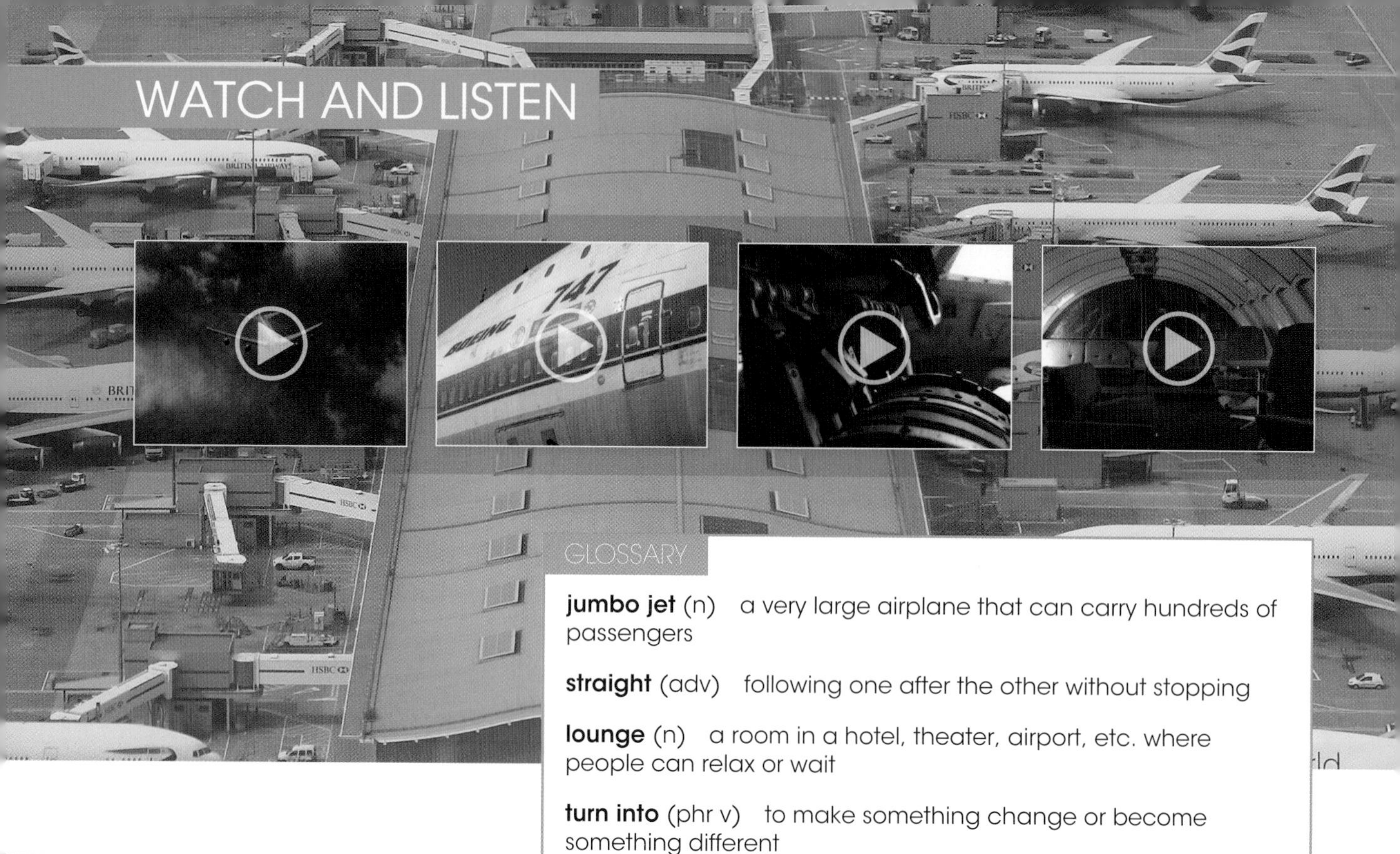

GLOSSARY

jumbo jet (n) a very large airplane that can carry hundreds of passengers

straight (adv) following one after the other without stopping

lounge (n) a room in a hotel, theater, airport, etc. where people can relax or wait

turn into (phr v) to make something change or become something different

PREPARING TO WATCH

1 ACTIVATING YOUR KNOWLEDGE **You are going to watch a video about airplanes. Before you watch, work with a partner and discuss the questions.**

1 What is the biggest airplane you have ever been on?
2 What is the longest flight you have ever taken?
3 How many hours do you think an airplane can fly without stopping?

2 PREDICTING CONTENT USING VISUALS **Work with a partner. Look at the photos from the video and discuss the questions.**

1 How old do you think this airplane is?
2 What did people probably use the room in the fourth picture for?
3 What are the differences between first class and regular/coach class on airplanes today?

WHILE WATCHING

3 UNDERSTANDING MAIN IDEAS **Watch the video. Complete the summary on page 67 with words in the box.**

changed	flew	had	helped	worked

In 1969, the first 747 (1) ________________ across the Atlantic Ocean. Jimmy Barber (2) ________________ build the first 747. He and his team (3) ________________ for many hours a day to complete it. The first 747 (4) ________________ two floors, with a lounge on the second floor. The 747 (5) ________________ air travel forever.

4 UNDERSTANDING DETAILS **Watch the video again. Circle the correct answer.**

1 The ability to carry enough ______ changed air travel.
a people b fuel c baggage

2 Today, many airplanes can travel for ______ hours without stopping.
a 8 b 12 c 14

3 The first 747s could carry about ______ people.
a 500 b 747 c 1,000

4 The ______ of air travel today is much lower than it was 50 years ago.
a cost b speed c comfort

CRITICAL THINKING

5 Work with a partner. Discuss the questions.

APPLY
What is your favorite kind of transportation? Why?

ANALYZE
What are the advantages of air travel?

ANALYZE
What are its disadvantages?

COLLABORATION

6 A Work in a small group. Complete the chart with one advantage and one disadvantage for each kind of transportation.

1 car		
2 train		
3 bus		
4 bike		
5 boat		

B Compare your answers with another group. Did any answers surprise you?

UNIT 4

CUSTOMS AND TRADITIONS

LEARNING OBJECTIVES

Key Reading Skill	Annotating
Additional Reading Skills	Understanding key vocabulary; using your knowledge; taking notes; reading for main ideas; making inferences; previewing; reading for details; synthesizing
Language Development	Avoiding generalizations; adverbs of frequency to avoid generalizations; synonyms to avoid repetition

ACTIVATE YOUR KNOWLEDGE

Work with a partner. Discuss the questions.

1. Which celebration is shown in the photo? Is there a similar event in your country?
2. What traditional celebrations do you have in your culture?
3. Which countries have you visited? What surprised you about the customs or traditions of the places you visited?

READING 1

PREPARING TO READ

1 UNDERSTANDING KEY VOCABULARY **You are going to read an article about customs and traditions in different countries. Before you read the article, read the definitions below. Complete the sentences with the correct form of the words in bold.**

appearance (n) the way someone or something looks

culture (n) a society with its own ideas, traditions, and ways of behaving

exchange (v) to give something to someone, and receive something that they give you

expect (v) to think that something will or should happen

formal (adj) correct or conservative in style, dress, or speech; not casual

greet (v) to welcome someone with particular words or actions

relationship (n) the way two people or groups feel and behave toward each other

1 I love traveling because I enjoy experiencing other ________________ and their food, celebrations, and traditions.
2 In many traditional wedding ceremonies, it's usual for the bride and groom to ________________ rings.
3 In Korea and some Spanish-speaking countries, people do not ________________ a woman to change her last name when she gets married.
4 In Thailand, people ________________ each other by holding their hands together, bowing, and saying "Sawadee," which is similar to "Hello" or "Good day" in English.
5 Many languages have two ways to say *you*. They have a ________________ word to use in polite situations like work and a different word for family and friends.
6 On their wedding day, most brides spend a lot of time and effort on their ________________. They want every detail of their hair, clothes, and makeup to be perfect.
7 In most cultures, people who have a close ________________ enjoy spending time together and giving each other gifts.

2 USING YOUR KNOWLEDGE **What "rules" do visitors to your country need to know in order to be polite? Write notes in the chart.**

custom / behavior	rules
greeting (kissing, shaking hands, etc.)	
giving gifts	
behavior in business meetings	
business dress code	
punctuality	

3 **Work in a small group. Discuss the following questions.**

1 Share the information from your charts. Which "rules" from your charts are similar? Which are different?

2 The article discusses correct behavior in Brazil, Japan, and India. What do you know about the unique customs of these countries?

Why learn about cultures before travel–
- know what to expect
- avoid misunderstandings

1 In recent decades foreign travel has become a multi-billion dollar industry. International travel has many benefits, but tourists can run into trouble if they don't take the time to learn about the **cultures** they're visiting. It is very important for travelers to take the time to learn about the cultures they are visiting so that they know what to **expect** and how to avoid cultural misunderstandings. That is why we are presenting this "Customs Around the World" series, where we will look at three different cultures every month to help you become a well-informed traveler. This month's exciting destinations are Brazil, Japan, and India.

Brazil– friendly, informal; greetings important

2 **Brazil** In general, Brazilian culture is informal. Most Brazilians are very friendly people, so it is important to say hello and goodbye to everyone. Women kiss men and each other on the cheek, but men usually just shake hands. Brazilians typically stand very close to each other and touch each other's arms, elbows, and back regularly while speaking. You should not move away if this happens. If you go to a business meeting, you are not expected to take a gift. In fact, an expensive gift can be seen as suspicious[1].

3 On the other hand, if you are invited to someone's house, you should take a gift—for example, flowers or chocolate. However, stay clear of anything purple or black, as these colors are related to death.

4 If you are invited to dinner, arrive at least 30 minutes late, but always dress well, because a person's **appearance** is very important to Brazilians.

5 **Japan** The Japanese are quite different from the Brazilians. They can be quite **formal**, so don't stand too close. Kissing or touching other people in public is not common. When you meet Japanese people, they may shake your hand, although bowing is the more traditional greeting.

6 In a business meeting, the Japanese often like to know what your position is in your company before they talk to you. You should hand over a business card using both hands, and when you receive a business card, you should immediately read it carefully. It is important to be punctual[2] in Japan. You should arrive early and dress formally. Gifts are often **exchanged**, but the recipient may refuse the gift at least once before accepting it. You should remember to do the same if you receive a gift. When you present your gift, you should say that it is just a token of your appreciation[3].

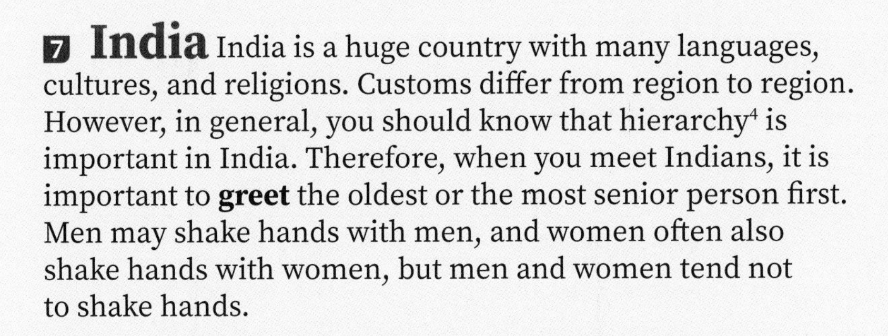

7 **India** India is a huge country with many languages, cultures, and religions. Customs differ from region to region. However, in general, you should know that hierarchy[4] is important in India. Therefore, when you meet Indians, it is important to **greet** the oldest or the most senior person first. Men may shake hands with men, and women often also shake hands with women, but men and women tend not to shake hands.

8 Personal **relationships** are important in business in India, and you should not be surprised if the first meeting is spent getting to know everyone. In addition, it is important to know that many Indians do not like to say "no," so it may be difficult to know what they are really thinking. Appointments are necessary, and punctuality is important. Business dress is formal, so men and women should wear dark suits.

9 If you are invited to an Indian's home, arrive on time. You do not have to bring a gift, but gifts are not refused. However, do not bring white flowers, because these are used in funerals[5].

[1]suspicious (adj) causing a feeling of distrust or that something is wrong

[2]punctual (adj) on time

[3]token of your appreciation (n) an inexpensive gift meant to express thanks or gratitude

[4]hierarchy (n) status; a system for organizing people according to their importance

[5]funeral (n) the ceremony held after someone has died

WHILE READING

SKILLS

ANNOTATING

Active readers annotate while reading. Use a system that you find easy to use and understand. Below are some suggestions:

- Highlight the main ideas in a bright color or put brackets ([ ]) around them.
- Highlight key words and phrases in a different color. Use colors consistently.
- Underline, circle, or box important details such as examples, reasons, and supporting arguments. In the margin, identify the type of detail you marked.

Also, as you read, write notes in the margins: summarize main ideas, list important supporting details, write any questions you have, and write your opinion or your reaction. Interacting with the text in this way will help you learn and remember the important information.

4 ANNOTATING **Read the article on pages 72–73. Annotate the text while you read. Part of the text has been annotated as an example.**

5 TAKING NOTES **Complete the student's notes with words and phrases from the article.**

custom/behavior	Brazil	Japan	India
greeting	Women (1)__________ other women & men. Men (2)__________ other men.	OK to (3)__________, but (4)__________ is more traditional.	Greet (5)__________ person first. Women shake hands with (6)__________, men with (7)__________.
gifts	Bring a gift to someone's (8)__________.	Receiving: (9)__________ before you accept. Giving: Say it is just a (10)__________.	Not (11)__________, but do not bring (12)__________.
business behavior	Do not bring a (13)__________.	Hand over your business card with (14)__________. When you receive a business card, (15)__________.	(16)__________ meeting spent getting to know everyone. Many Indians do not like to say (17)__________. (18)__________ are necessary.
dress/appearance	Dress (19)__________.	Dress (20)__________.	Business dress is (21)__________.
punctuality	Arrive (22)__________.	Arrive (23)__________.	Arrive (24)__________.

6 READING FOR MAIN IDEAS **Read the article again. Circle the customs that are not mentioned in the article.**

a greetings
b personal space
c giving gifts
d business meetings
e table manners
f giving business cards
g being punctual

READING BETWEEN THE LINES

7 MAKING INFERENCES **Work with a partner. Answer the questions.**

1 In Brazil, why would people probably be suspicious of an expensive gift?

____

2 Why shouldn't you move away if Brazilians touch you during conversation?

____

3 Why would Japanese businesspeople want to know your position in a company?

____

4 What could be the reason why Indians don't like to say "no"?

____

5 What can be the negative result of a cultural misunderstanding?

____

CRITICAL THINKING

8 **Work with a partner. Discuss the questions.**

UNDERSTAND	APPLY	EVALUATE
Which customs are similar in Brazil, Japan, and India? Which are different?	Which of these countries would you most like to visit? Why?	Have you ever made a cultural mistake in a foreign country? Describe it.

COLLABORATION

9 **A** Work in a small group. Describe at least three interesting customs from other cultures. Think about the topics in the reading or any of the following:

- Money
- Love
- Tipping
- Gender roles
- Meals and food
- Respect for older people

B As a group, choose the most interesting customs and present them to the class. Each person should present one custom.

READING 2

PREPARING TO READ

1 UNDERSTANDING KEY VOCABULARY **You are going to read an article about nontraditional weddings. Before you read the article, read the definitions below. Complete the sentences with the correct form of the words in bold.**

belief (n) an idea that you are certain is true

ceremony (n) a formal event with special traditions, activities, or words, such as a wedding

couple (n) two people who are married or in a relationship

engaged (adj) having a formal agreement to get married

reception (n) a formal party that is given to celebrate a special event or to welcome someone

relative (n) any member of your family

theme (n) the main idea, subject, or topic of an event, book, musical piece, etc.

1 In Mexican culture, a *quinceñera* is a special ________________ to celebrate a girl's fifteenth birthday.

2 A honeymoon is a time for a newly married ________________ to relax after the wedding and spend time alone.

3 Children tend to have the same ________________ as their parents when they are young, but this may change when they become adults.

4 My sister and her boyfriend became ______________ on New Year's Eve, and their wedding will be after they both graduate from college.

5 My sister loves 80s music, so we're having an 80s ______________ for her birthday celebration.

6 My cousin's wedding took place in city hall, and the ______________ afterwards was held in a hotel.

7 I have a large family with many aunts, uncles, and cousins. It's fun to get together with all my ______________ on special occasions.

2 PREVIEWING **Work with a partner. Look at the title and the photos on pages 78–79 and answer the questions.**

1 What is happening in the photos? Where do you think they were taken?

____

2 Is this type of thing becoming more popular in your country or culture?

____

3 How would your family react if you decided to have a wedding like the couples in the photos?

____

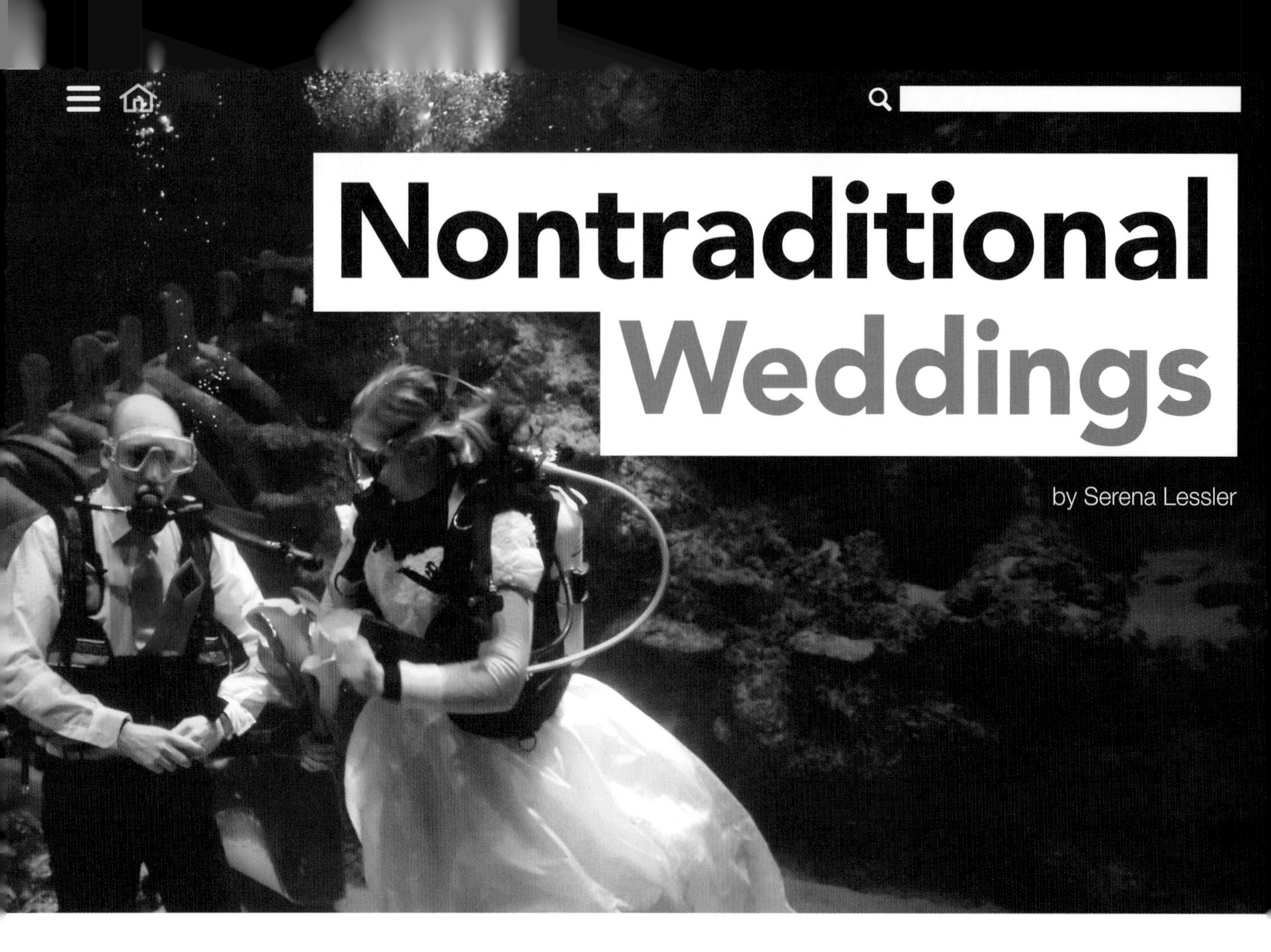

Nontraditional Weddings

by Serena Lessler

1 Even if they have never attended a traditional American wedding in person, most people have probably seen such weddings in movies or on television. The beautiful bride in her white dress, the handsome groom, the **ceremony** in the church, the romantic music—these customs are familiar to people all over the world. Though most American **couples** still choose to have this kind of traditional wedding, more and more couples these days are planning unique weddings that reflect their **beliefs**, hobbies, and personal style. Three types of nontraditional weddings are adventure weddings, destination weddings, and **theme** weddings.

---

2 Adventure weddings typically combine the marriage ceremony with a physical activity that has special meaning for the couple. Cathy and Frank Mason, enthusiastic scuba divers who had participated in dives all over the world, met on a shark-diving adventure near Key West, Florida, in 2012. A year later they were **engaged** and were starting to plan their wedding. Cathy had always dreamed of a large, traditional wedding in a church, but from the start Frank had a different idea. Why not have a wedding that combined their love for each other and the activity they loved most—scuba diving? Cathy finally agreed, and the couple were married underwater in May, 2015—surrounded by numerous friends and **relatives**, all in scuba gear. Other adventure-seeking couples have been known to get married while water skiing, skydiving, or riding in a hot-air balloon.

3 Most people are less adventurous than the Masons, but many of them love to travel. It is becoming more and more common for such couples to get married in a distant location. An American couple, Arielle Cogan and Richard Thompson, met when both of them were spending a year studying history in Edinburgh, Scotland. After they became engaged, they discovered that neither of them was interested in an ordinary wedding. Instead, they were married in a small, 18th-century church in Edinburgh with just their families and a few close friends as guests. The bride wore a traditional white dress and the groom wore a kilt, which is a traditional Scottish skirt for men! Destination weddings allow couples to get married in the place of their dreams. The main disadvantage is the cost: It can be expensive to have family and friends fly to an exotic location on the other side of the world.

---

4 A theme wedding allows couples to create a fun, nontraditional wedding that centers around a beloved book, song, story, or historical period. A couple from Epping, New Hampshire, planned every detail of their wedding, from the wedding vows to the food at the **reception**, around the theme of the Harry Potter books by J.K. Rowling. Other unique themes for weddings have included pirates, superheroes like Superman, a Hawaiian luau, country music, Victorian England, the 1960s, a fairy tale like "Cinderella," and many, many more.

> **"Couples these days are free to choose almost any type of wedding they can imagine.**

5 Unlike the past, when a traditional religious wedding was the only option available to marrying couples, couples these days are free to choose almost any type of wedding they can imagine. The variety of wedding styles and locations is perhaps a reflection of the general trend toward individual choice and self expression that has been growing stronger in the U.S. since the 1960s. But whether a couple chooses an old-fashioned church wedding or a ceremony at the top of a mountain, the central purpose of a wedding—to celebrate the union of a couple in the presence of the people who love them—has not changed, and it probably never will.

WHILE READING

3 ANNOTATING **Read the article on pages 78–79 and annotate the text. Look at page 74 for what to annotate.**

4 READING FOR MAIN IDEAS **Use your notes and annotations for Reading 2 to put the following main ideas in the order they were discussed in the article.**

theme weddings ____

adventure weddings ____

reasons for the popularity of nontraditional weddings ____

destination weddings ____

choices for couples who want a nontraditional wedding ____

5 **Circle the best summary of the article's main idea.**

a The text describes a traditional American wedding and gives examples of nontraditional weddings.

b The text contrasts traditional and modern relationships in the United States.

c The text describes marriage customs around the world.

d The text describes a religious wedding in the United States.

6 READING FOR DETAILS **Correct the factual mistakes in the sentences.**

1 In a traditional wedding, the bride wears a white suit.

____

2 Frank Mason wanted a traditional wedding in a church.

____

3 Destination weddings take place close to the bride and groom's home.

____

4 Getting married underwater is a kind of theme wedding.

____

5 The couple from Epping, New Hampshire, had an adventure wedding.

____

6 Today there are few options for couples who want a nontraditional wedding.

____

READING BETWEEN THE LINES

7 MAKING INFERENCES **Work with a partner. Answer the questions.**

1 These days, do most American couples choose to have traditional or nontraditional weddings? Why?

____

2 What might be the disadvantages of an adventure wedding or a theme wedding?

____

3 What kind of people might choose to have each type of wedding described in the article?

____

CRITICAL THINKING

8 SYNTHESIZING **Work with a partner. Use ideas from Reading 1 and Reading 2 to answer the questions.**

UNDERSTAND

Imagine that you are going to attend a wedding in Brazil, Japan, or India. How would you dress? What time should you arrive? What type of gift should you give? What type of gift would you avoid giving?

ANALYZE

Why do you think more American couples are choosing to have nontraditional weddings these days? Is this true in your country as well?

ANALYZE

Besides weddings, are any other traditional celebrations in your country changing? How?

COLLABORATION

9 **A** Work in a small group. Imagine that you are going to plan a wedding. Choose a traditional or nontraditional wedding. Discuss the following details and anything else that is important. Then create a wedding plan or schedule.

- Type
- Location
- Guests
- Decorations
- Clothing
- Music
- Food
- Accommodations

B Present your wedding plan to the class. As a class, vote on the wedding you would most like to attend.

LANGUAGE DEVELOPMENT

AVOIDING GENERALIZATIONS

LANGUAGE

In academic English, be careful not to make general statements unless you have the data to prove them. A reader of the example sentence below can argue that not all weddings are expensive.

Weddings are expensive.

You can avoid generalizations by using words such as *many, can*, or *tend to*.

Quantifier:	**Many** weddings are expensive.
Modal verb:	Weddings **can be** expensive.
Verb:	Weddings **tend to be** expensive.

1 Read the sentences. Use the words in parentheses to avoid generalizations.

1 We tip the waiter in restaurants. (tend to)

2 Formal weddings are less common these days. (tend to)

3 Anniversaries are important. (can)

4 Common hand gestures like waving are misunderstood in a different culture. (can)

5 In Mexico, old people live with their children. (most)

ADVERBS OF FREQUENCY TO AVOID GENERALIZATIONS

LANGUAGE

You can also use adverbs of frequency to avoid generalizations. They are:

0%					100%
never	seldom hardly ever rarely	occasionally sometimes	often	usually almost always normally	always

Notice the position of the adverbs in the sentences.

Before the main verb: People **usually** have barbecues in summer.

After the verb *to be*: Weddings are **often** difficult to organize.

2 Read the sentences. Use the adverbs in parentheses to avoid generalizations.

1 In the past, the bride's family paid for the wedding. (usually)

2 Outdoor weddings are cheaper than church weddings. (often)

3 Professionals get upset if you don't use their correct title. (sometimes)

4 Cultural knowledge is helpful in business situations. (frequently)

5 In Japan, you should arrive on time for an appointment. (always)

SYNONYMS TO AVOID REPETITION

3 Replace the words in bold in the sentences with the synonyms in the box.

brief	certain	common	important	obvious	separate	serious

1 The wedding was **short**, and we went straight to the reception.

____

2 The high cost of weddings is a **bad** problem for many families.

____

3 The bride and groom live in **different** houses until after the wedding.

____

4 In **some** countries, marriage is becoming less popular. ____________________

5 In the past, people often married into **powerful** families for money and status.

____

6 Some customs and traditions are not **clear** to people who are visiting a country for the first time. ____________________

7 It is **usual** for people in my country to have large families. ____________________

WATCH AND LISTEN

GLOSSARY

Halloween (n) a holiday on October 31st when children wear costumes, visit other houses, and say "trick or treat" to ask for candy

costume (n) a set of clothes that someone wears to make them look like someone or something else, e.g., in a play

pumpkin (n) a large, round vegetable with thick, orange skin

Celtic (adj) related to the ancient people of Ireland, Scotland, and Wales

retailer (n) a person or business that sells products to the public

PREPARING TO WATCH

1 ACTIVATING YOUR KNOWLEDGE **You are going to watch a video about Halloween. Before you watch, work with a partner and discuss the questions.**

1 Do people in your country ever wear costumes? Why?

2 Do people ever decorate their homes for special events? How?

3 Do people ever eat special foods to celebrate events and holidays? Which ones?

2 PREDICTING CONTENT USING VISUALS **Work with a partner. Look at the photos from the video and discuss the questions.**

1 What do people do on Halloween?

2 What is the girl looking at in the store?

WHILE WATCHING

3 UNDERSTANDING MAIN IDEAS **Watch the video. Circle the correct answer.**

1 On Halloween people eat a lot of *candy* / *pumpkins*.

2 Many people wear *scarves* / *costumes* on Halloween.

3 Halloween is based on an old Celtic *religion* / *tradition*.

4 Retailers think Halloween is *good* / *not good* for business.

5 The average *person* / *retailer* spends about $75 on Halloween.

4 UNDERSTANDING DETAILS **Watch the video again. Write *T* (true), *F* (false), or *DNS* (does not say) next to the statements. Then, correct the false statements.**

_____ 1 Tens of billions of trick-or-treaters celebrate Halloween.

_____ 2 The most expensive variety of candy is chocolate.

_____ 3 Illinois produces the most Halloween costumes.

_____ 4 U.S. retailers make more money on Christmas than Halloween.

_____ 5 Halloween is celebrated in many countries.

5 MAKING INFERENCES **Work with a partner and discuss the questions. Give reasons for your answers.**

1 Is Halloween more popular with children or adults? Why?

2 Why do people dress in costumes on Halloween?

3 During which holiday in the United States do people spend the most money?

CRITICAL THINKING

6 **Work with a partner. Discuss the questions.**

APPLY

Have you ever worn a costume for Halloween or for another special occasion? Describe it.

APPLY

Do people in your country celebrate Halloween? Why or why not?

EVALUATE

Why might some Americans not want to celebrate Halloween?

COLLABORATION

7 **A** Choose a holiday to research. For example:

- Martin Luther King Day
- April Fool's Day
- Father's Day
- Valentine's Day
- Memorial Day
- Kwanzaa

Find photos and information about the holiday. Think about:

- How did it start?
- How do people celebrate it?
- When is it?
- What do you like most about it?
- Who celebrates it?

B Work in a small group. Present your holiday to the group.

C Choose one holiday to present to the class.

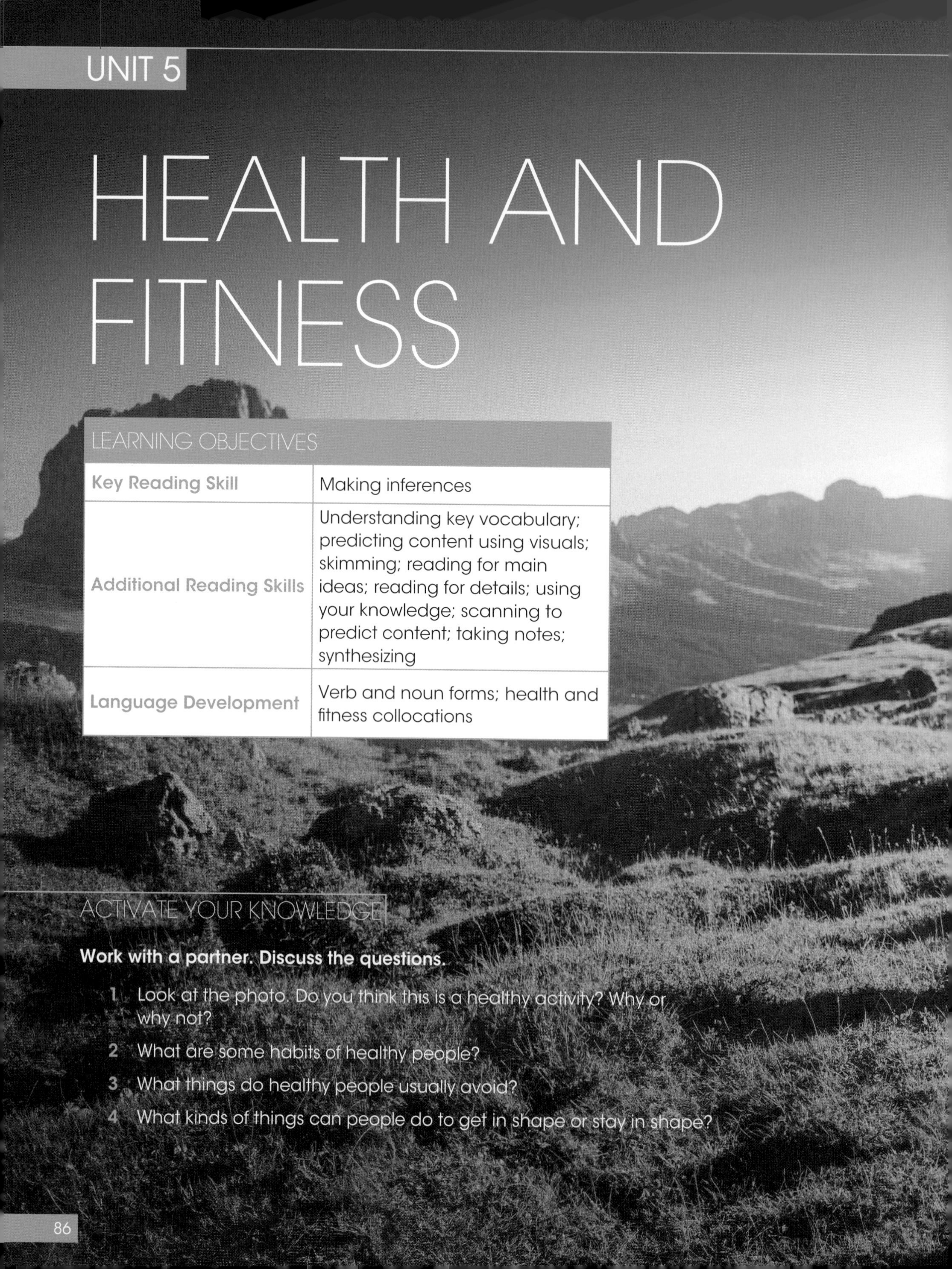

UNIT 5

HEALTH AND FITNESS

LEARNING OBJECTIVES

Key Reading Skill	Making inferences
Additional Reading Skills	Understanding key vocabulary; predicting content using visuals; skimming; reading for main ideas; reading for details; using your knowledge; scanning to predict content; taking notes; synthesizing
Language Development	Verb and noun forms; health and fitness collocations

ACTIVATE YOUR KNOWLEDGE

Work with a partner. Discuss the questions.

1. Look at the photo. Do you think this is a healthy activity? Why or why not?
2. What are some habits of healthy people?
3. What things do healthy people usually avoid?
4. What kinds of things can people do to get in shape or stay in shape?

READING 1

PREPARING TO READ

1 UNDERSTANDING KEY VOCABULARY **Read the sentences. Complete the definitions with the words in bold.**

1. Type 2 diabetes is an extremely **serious** condition. Many people die each year from the complications of this illness.
2. Participation in sports is an excellent way to raise the **self-esteem** of teenagers. It helps them to feel confident and happy with themselves.
3. My grandmother is 88 years old, but she is still quite **active**. She walks every day and even plays tennis twice a week.
4. To lose weight, you should get more exercise and eat fewer **calories**.
5. To stay healthy you should do a **moderate** amount of exercise each week. Two and a half hours a week is the right amount.
6. Many young people do not **recognize** the importance of getting enough sleep.
7. I have decided to **reduce** the amount of sugar I eat. Now I have dessert only once a week.

a ______________ (adj) doing things that involve movement and energy

b ______________ (v) to limit; to use less of something

c ______________ (adj) bad or dangerous

d ______________ (n) a feeling of confidence and pride in yourself

e ______________ (n) measurement of the amount of energy found in food

f ______________ (v) to understand; to accept that something is true

g ______________ (adj) not too much and not too little

2 PREDICTING CONTENT USING VISUALS **Write the names of the types of exercise shown in the photos.**

a ____________ b ____________ c ____________ d ____________

e ____________ f ____________ g ____________ h ____________

1 How much physical activity do you do in a week? Are you getting enough exercise? Regular activity benefits your health in many ways. For example, people who exercise regularly are less likely to suffer from many chronic diseases[1], such as heart disease, type 2 diabetes[2], stroke[3], and some cancers. Experts say adults who exercise for just 150 minutes a week can **reduce** their risk of **serious** illness by 50%. In addition, regular exercise increases life expectancy[4] and reduces the risk of early death by 30%. It also improves your mood, **self-esteem**, and sleep quality.

2 Today, most adults are much less **active** than in the past, because our jobs are far less physical than the work our grandparents used to do. In fact, many of us spend seven hours or more just sitting in a chair each day. This lack of regular physical activity means that people burn fewer **calories** than in the past, so we need to make an extra effort to use up all our energy. According to experts, adults need to do two and a half hours of **moderate** exercise per week. This could be fast walking or cycling on a flat road. In addition, it is important to do exercises to strengthen muscles two or three times a week.

3 Exercise can be expensive, but it doesn't have to be. Team sports such as soccer or basketball can be cheap, because all the players share the cost of the field or court. Joining a recreational sports league is usually an inexpensive way of getting exercise and can be very social, too. Local recreation centers usually offer racquetball at low rates if you book a court at off-peak times, and you may be able to get a reduced-price gym membership, too.

4 If you don't want to spend any money at all, try one of the following

activities. Go for a run; the only equipment you need is a pair of running shoes. If you take the bus, try getting off one stop early and walking the extra distance. Go to the park. Try getting a group of friends or family together for a game of soccer, or play the kinds of running games you haven't played since you were a child. This is a great way to involve the whole family and also help you get in shape. Alternatively, if you want to stay at home, gardening or doing housework are great ways to get in shape, and you can enjoy the benefit of a nice garden and a tidy house, too!

5 Although adults should do two and a half hours of exercise a week, you don't have to do it all at one time. Split the time into ten-minute chunks! If you do ten minutes before work, ten minutes during your lunch break and ten minutes after work, five days a week, you've achieved the target! You could also go swimming during your lunch hour two or three times a week and you've done it! In brief, there are many easy ways of getting in shape. If we all **recognize** the value of doing this, we will live longer and be healthier.

[1]**chronic disease** (n) a disease that lasts a long time

[2]**diabetes** (n) a disease in which the body is not able to use sugar efficiently

[3]**stroke** (n) a medical condition in which blood cannot reach the brain and the brain becomes damaged

[4]**life expectancy** (n) the number of years that a person can expect to live

WHILE READING

3 SKIMMING **Skim the article on pages 90–91, and circle the best title.**

a Exercising to Lose Weight

b Walking to Improve Health and Mood

c Staying in Shape—It's Easier than You Think

d Exercise Every Day to Keep the Doctor Away

4 READING FOR MAIN IDEAS **Read the article. Match the headings to the paragraphs in the article. There is one extra heading that you do not need.**

a If you can't afford gym membership... ______

b Exercise regularly to stay healthy. ______

c Think you don't have time? ______

d Swimming is the best form of exercise. ______

e Get out of your chair. ______

f Exercise can be free. ______

5 READING FOR DETAILS **Read the article again and answer the questions.**

1 Which four medical problems can be avoided with regular exercise?

______, ______, ______, ______

2 Which other three things does exercise improve?

______, ______, ______

3 How much time do some adults spend each day sitting down?

______

4 What do team sport players share the cost of? ______

5 When should you book a racquetball court for cheap rates?

______

6 What equipment do you need for running? ______

7 Where should you go to exercise and spend time with your family?

______

READING BETWEEN THE LINES

SKILLS

MAKING INFERENCES

Making inferences means using your knowledge and clues in the text to guess about things that aren't stated in the text but are probably true. For example:

After two miles, Amir could not run another step, but Danya kept going.

Question: Who is in better shape, Amir or Danya? **Answer:** Danya

We can tell Danya is in better shape because she "kept going" and Amir "could not run another step."

Readers make inferences about the people in a text (age, attitude, feelings, etc.). They also make inferences about the writer's purpose, intention, background, or attitude.

6 MAKING INFERENCES **Review the article and answer the questions.**

1 How do you think exercise improves self-esteem?

____

2 What do you think is the relationship between regular exercise and life expectancy?

____

3 Is the fact sheet written for adults or for children? How do you know?

____

CRITICAL THINKING

7 **Work with a partner. Discuss the questions.**

APPLY

Are sports the best way to keep fit? Why or why not?

ANALYZE

Which sports or physical activities are the healthiest?

EVALUATE

Is exercise ever a bad thing? Why or why not?

COLLABORATION

8 **A** Work with a partner. Make a survey about fitness activities. Add at least two questions to the list below.

- What do you do to stay in shape?
- How many hours a week do you do it?
- What are its benefits?
- How long have you been doing it?
- Do you think you are active enough, or would you like to be more active?

B Survey three people, and report your results to the class.

C As a class, summarize the survey results on the board.

READING 2

PREPARING TO READ

1 UNDERSTANDING KEY VOCABULARY **Read the definitions. Complete the sentences with the correct form of the words in bold.**

balanced diet (n) a daily eating program that has a healthy mixture of different kinds of food

campaign (n) a group of activities designed to motivate people to take action, such as giving money or changing their behavior

junk food (n) food that is unhealthy but quick and easy to eat

nutritional (adj) relating to food and the way it affects your health

obesity (n) the condition of being extremely overweight

portion (n) an amount of food served to one person

1 I try to eat a ________________ consisting of a little meat, some dairy products, and a lot of fruit, vegetables, and grains.

2 I love ________________ like potato chips and hot dogs, but I'm careful not to eat too much of those foods because I know they aren't good for me.

3 ________________ is a serious problem all over the world. In some countries, more than 50% of adults are overweight.

4 One way to lose weight is to eat the same foods but smaller ________________.

5 Right now, my company is sponsoring a ________________ to raise money for a new gym in the local school.

6 Snacks like candy and potato chips have little ________________ value. Having fruit or raw vegetables is much better for your body.

2 USING YOUR KNOWLEDGE **Work with a partner. Answer the questions.**

1 What percentage of your diet is
   a fruit and vegetables? ______
   b carbohydrates? ______
   c dairy products? ______
   d proteins? ______
2 What percentage of your diet should be
   a fruit and vegetables? ______
   b carbohydrates? ______
   c dairy products? ______
   d proteins? ______
3 How can governments help people avoid obesity?

______

3 SCANNING TO PREDICT CONTENT **Scan the essay on pages 96–97 and check your answers to questions 2 and 3 in Exercise 2.**

TACKLING OBESITY

Figure 1 A healthy, balanced diet

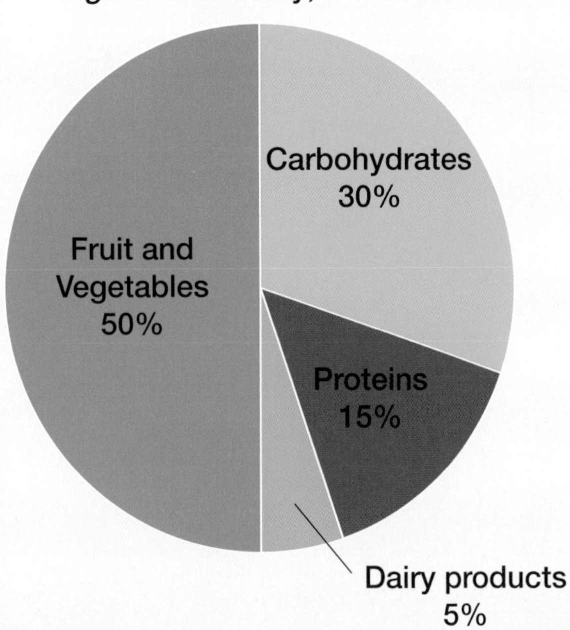

1 **Obesity** is becoming a major problem in many parts of the world. In the United States, the number of obese adults has more than doubled over the past 25 years. Nearly 70% of American adults are overweight or obese. Obesity can cause major health problems like heart disease, diabetes, stroke, and breathing problems. Experts estimate that in the United States alone, 1 in 5 deaths are linked to obesity—that is almost 300,000 deaths per year. Tackling[1] obesity is a big task. In my opinion, it should be the shared responsibility of individuals, governments, and the media.

2 First, individuals need to do their part to make sure they stay healthy. One way for people to fight obesity is to eat smaller **portions** and to eat more healthfully. An average man needs around 2,500 calories per day, while an average woman requires around 2,000. We should eat a **balanced diet** that consists of a variety of foods in order to maintain a healthy weight. A healthy diet should include approximately 50% fruit and vegetables; 30% carbohydrates, such as bread, rice, potatoes, and pasta; 15% proteins, for example, meat, fish, eggs, and beans; and

around 5% dairy products, such as milk and cheese. Very little should be sweet foods like candy or cookies.

3 Governments around the world must also do their part to fight obesity in their countries. In many countries, laws require food packaging to show accurate **nutritional** information. In addition, large restaurant chains in the United States must list calorie counts for items on their menus. These restaurants must also provide additional written nutritional information about fat, sodium[2], and cholesterol[3] amounts if a customer asks for it. This information helps people better understand the nutritional value of the food they eat, even when they are not cooking at home or eating packaged food. Some countries tax foods that are high in fat, such as pizza and potato chips, and those high in refined sugar[4], like chocolate and candy. This makes **junk food** too expensive for people to buy in large quantities. In some countries, there is now a tax on products that contain more than a certain percentage of saturated fat[5].

4 Moreover, the role of the media and advertising should not be overlooked. Advertising junk food at times when children are watching TV was banned in Malaysia in 2007. This action was designed to protect children from the influence of advertising while they learn how to choose between treats and foods that are good for them. There have also been several educational **campaigns** on TV to encourage people to eat five portions of fruit and vegetables per day. It has been estimated that if people ate enough fruits and vegetables, up to 2.7 million lives per year could be saved.

5 To summarize, individuals, governments, and the media all need to do their part to reduce obesity in our society. Individuals should take responsibility for their meal choices and choose healthier foods in smaller portions. At the same time, governments should take action and pass laws that encourage healthier lifestyles. The media can also play a role by teaching people about healthier eating habits and not advertising junk food to children. I believe that if individuals, governments, and the media all do their part, then perhaps we can see an end to obesity in the near future.

[1]**tackle** (v) to deal with something

[2]**sodium** (n) the main chemical element found in salt

[3]**cholesterol** (n) a fatty substance found in all animal cells. A high level can block arteries and may cause heart disease.

[4]**refined sugar** (n) white table sugar, which has been processed in a factory, as opposed to the natural sugar found in fruit or honey

[5]**saturated** fat (n) unhealthful fats that contain higher proportions of fatty acid

WHILE READING

4 READING FOR MAIN IDEAS **Read the essay on pages 96–97. Match the paragraphs of the essay to the themes. You will list one paragraph twice.**

a the government's role ________
b how to have a healthy diet ________
c nutritional information ________
d an introduction to the obesity problem ________
e the role of advertising ________
f an end to obesity ________

5 TAKING NOTES **Read paragraphs 2–5 of the essay again. Underline the solutions to tackling obesity, and highlight their purposes. Then take notes on the purpose of each solution in the chart.**

solutions to tackle obesity	purpose
a balanced diet	1 to maintain a healthy weight
packaging labels	2
a food tax	3
a ban on junk food advertising to children	4
education campaigns	5

6 READING FOR DETAILS **Read the essay again to look for the examples that the author uses to add detail to the argument. Write at least two examples for each topic.**

1 carbohydrates ________________ ________________
2 dairy products ________________ ________________
3 proteins ________________ ________________
4 sweet foods ________________ ________________
5 high-fat foods ________________ ________________
6 sugary foods ________________ ________________

READING BETWEEN THE LINES

7 MAKING INFERENCES **Work with a partner. Answer the questions.**

1 Why does the author think that obesity is a serious problem?

____

2 Following the information in the text, give an example of a balanced meal that you ate recently.

____

3 How does nutritional information on food packaging and in restaurants help people eat more healthfully?

____

4 Why do you think the government of Malaysia decided to ban junk food advertisements to children? What information did they probably use to support this decision?

____

CRITICAL THINKING

8 SYNTHESIZING **Work with a partner. Use ideas from Reading 1 and Reading 2 to answer the questions.**

ANALYZE

Which is more important for good health: a regular exercise program or a balanced diet? Why?

EVALUATE

Many people work hard and get a lot of exercise in their jobs, but they are still obese. Why do you think that happens?

COLLABORATION

9 **A** As a class, choose one of the following statements to debate.

- *Advertisements for junk food should be made illegal.*
- *Governments should tax products that are bad for our health.*
- *It's up to individuals to control their weight. Government should not be involved.*

Divide the class into two groups: one group will argue in favor of the idea and the other will argue against it. Prepare your arguments.

B Have a class debate. Take turns speaking so that everyone has a chance to speak. Take notes on the opposing side's arguments and prepare counter-arguments. Your teacher will decide the winner.

LANGUAGE DEVELOPMENT

VERB AND NOUN FORMS

LANGUAGE

It is important to recognize both the verb and the noun form of words when you are reading, and to spell them correctly when you are writing.

Notice: Sometimes the verb and noun forms are the same.

The biggest thing that stops people going to the gym is the **cost**. (noun)
Gym membership should **cost** less so more people can join. (verb)

1 Look at the verbs in the box and underline their noun forms in the paragraph.

advertise	ban	encourage	promote
protect	recognize	reduce	

We need to see a reduction in the rate of obesity among young people. The first step is recognition that fat is a real problem for young people. One solution is for schools to offer children the opportunity to participate in sports. This would require the involvement and encouragement of parents, who are our main weapon against increasing obesity. Parents can also support the promotion of educational campaigns to teach children about healthy eating.

All of us should be responsible for the protection of our own health, but governments can also help fight the obesity epidemic. For example, they can impose a ban on junk food advertisements that target children.

HEALTH AND FITNESS COLLOCATIONS

LANGUAGE

Collocations are pairs of words that frequently occur together, for example, noun + noun or adjective + noun. Collocations sound correct to fluent speakers of a language. For example, *heart disease* is a frequent collocation in English. It sounds correct. On the other hand, *heart illness* sounds wrong, even though we can understand the meaning.

2 Look at the paragraph and underline ten collocations (noun + noun or adjective + noun) related to health and fitness. The first one has been done for you as an example.

Obesity can reduce life expectancy and lead to serious illness such as heart disease and diabetes. To address this problem, some governments run educational programs and advertising campaigns. These educate people about the dangers of junk food and the importance of a balanced diet. They also show people how to find out about the nutritional value of food. Another important way to tackle obesity is regular exercise, because the more physical activity we have, the better we feel.

3 Now complete the chart by writing the correct collocation next to the definition.

definition	collocation
how long a person can expect to live	1 life expectancy
how good a particular kind of food is for you	2
classes or material to teach people about a particular topic	3
an illness of the heart	4
moving around and doing things	5
media projects to convince people to buy a product or change their behavior	6
a very bad medical problem	7
a mixture of the correct types and amounts of food	8
sports or movement that people do at the same time each day, week, month, etc.	9
food that is unhealthy but is quick and easy to eat	10

WATCH AND LISTEN

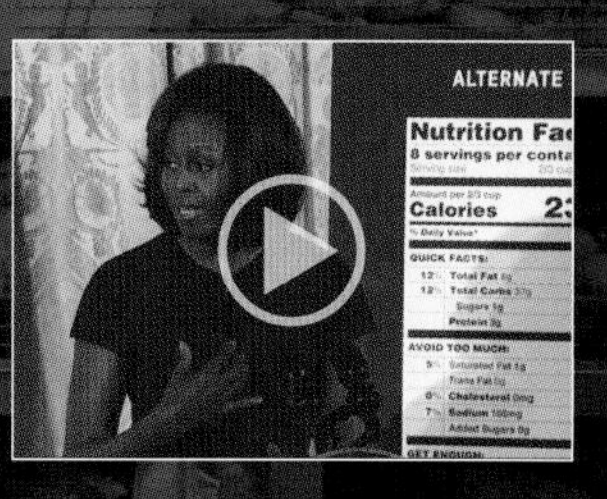

GLOSSARY

nutrition label (n) a chart on a package of food that gives information about how the food might affect your health

Food and Drug Administration (n) FDA; the U.S. government agency that makes sure food and medicine is safe for people to use

serving size (n) the amount of a food or drink one person normally eats or drinks at one meal

beverage (n) a drink of any type

consumer (n) someone who buys goods or services for personal use

PREPARING TO WATCH

1 ACTIVATING YOUR KNOWLEDGE **You are going to watch a video about nutrition. Before you watch, work with a partner and discuss the questions.**

1 What do you often eat for a snack?
2 Which snack foods are healthy and which are unhealthy?
3 What information on a nutrition label is important to you?

2 PREDICTING CONTENT USING VISUALS **Work with a partner. Look at the photos from the video and discuss the questions.**

1 Which of these foods do you think has the most calories?
2 What do you think the woman with the blond hair is doing in the first photo?
3 What could Michelle Obama be talking about?

WHILE WATCHING

3 UNDERSTANDING MAIN IDEAS **Watch the video. Match the sentence halves.**

1 The FDA wants to
2 The calories on food labels will
3 The serving size will
4 The new labels will
5 Changing food labels could

a be more realistic.
b list any added sugars.
c cost a lot of money.
d change the labels on food.
e be bigger and easier to read.

4 UNDERSTANDING DETAILS **Watch the video again. Answer the questions.**

1 When was the last time food labels were changed?

____

2 How will serving sizes change?

____

3 What have some beverage companies already done?

____

4 How much could it cost to produce new labels?

____

5 What does Michelle Obama think parents have a right to understand?

____

5 MAKING INFERENCES **Work with a partner. Discuss the questions and give reasons for your answers.**

1 Why would a food company not list added sugars?

2 Why would a food company list a serving size that is smaller than what someone usually eats or drinks?

3 Which of the following would Michelle Obama probably support?

- a healthier public school lunches
- b smaller labels on snack foods
- c higher taxes on beverages

CRITICAL THINKING

6 **Work in a small group. Discuss your answers.**

APPLY

What is the purpose of nutrition labels on food?

ANALYZE

What other products have special warning labels?

EVALUATE

How well do warning labels work?

COLLABORATION

7 **A** Work in a small group. What ingredients are in foods that you eat regularly? Make a list of five things you should eat more of and five things you could eat less of to become healthier.

B Compare your lists with the class. Vote on the top five ingredients to eat more of and the top five to eat less of.

UNIT 6

DISCOVERY AND INVENTION

LEARNING OBJECTIVES

Key Reading Skills	Scanning to find information; using a T-chart
Additional Reading Skills	Understanding key vocabulary; previewing; reading for main ideas; annotating; making inferences; using your knowledge; taking notes; reading for details; synthesizing
Language Development	Making predictions with modals and adverbs of certainty; prefixes

ACTIVATE YOUR KNOWLEDGE

Work with a partner. Discuss the questions.

1. Think of an invention from the last ten years. What does it do? What is its purpose? How does it help people? Does it have any disadvantages?
2. What do you think will happen in the world of science and technology in the next ten years?
3. If you could invent one thing to help the world, what would it be?

READING 1

PREPARING TO READ

1 UNDERSTANDING KEY VOCABULARY **Read the definitions. Complete the sentences with the correct form of the words in bold.**

essential (adj) very important or necessary

harmful (adj) able to hurt or damage

helpful (adj) useful

illustrate (v) to show the meaning or truth of something more clearly, especially by giving examples

pattern (n) a set of lines, colors, or shapes that repeat in a regular way

prevent (v) to stop something from happening or stop someone from doing something

unlimited (adj) without end or restriction

1 Before the invention of sunscreen, people had no way to protect themselves from the ________________ rays of the sun.
2 Many cooks say that the food processor was a ________________ invention because it saves a lot of preparation time in the kitchen.
3 The discovery of vaccines was extraordinarily important because they make it possible for us to ________________ millions of deaths from illnesses like polio and smallpox.
4 The planet Uranus has an interesting ________________ of stripes, which is visible by viewing the planet with a telescope.
5 The human brain has an almost ________________ memory capacity, far more than that of a computer.
6 If you want to be an engineer or a scientist, it's ________________ that you get a strong background in science and math.
7 The engineer used diagrams to ________________ his point about the mechanics of suspension bridges like the Golden Gate Bridge.

2 PREVIEWING **Work with a partner. Discuss the questions and write your answers in the blanks.**

1 *Bio-* is a prefix that means "life." What words do you know that start with *bio-*?

____

2 Read the title, the introduction, and the first paragraph of the article on pages 108–109. What do *mimicry* and *biomimicry* mean?

____

3 Can you think of any inventions that copy their shape or function from something in nature?

____

THE MAGIC OF MIMICRY

To *mimic* people means "to copy their speech, dress, or behavior." However, in science, *mimic* means "copying ideas from nature or natural processes to solve problems or to create **helpful** products." This is called *biomimicry*, and its influence can be seen in many everyday products.

1 Perhaps the best-known example of biomimicry is Velcro®. It was invented in 1941 by a Swiss engineer called George de Mestral. One day, Mestral noticed the burdock seeds that stuck to his dog's hair. Under the microscope, he discovered that these seeds had hooks on them, so they stuck to loops on clothing or hair. Mestral copied this idea and created two strips of material, one with tiny hooks and the other with loose loops. When he put both strips together, they stuck like glue. However, unlike with glue, he could peel the strips apart and reattach them. Velcro® was initially unpopular with fashion companies, but after it was used by NASA to stop items from floating in space, it became popular with children's clothing companies. Today it is used to fasten everything from lunch bags to shoes.

2 More recently, swimwear has also been influenced by nature. The Speedo Fastskin®, a controversial swimsuit, was seen at the Beijing Olympics in 2008 and worn by 28 of the 33 gold medal winners. The technology is based on the rough **patterns** on a shark's skin, which allows the shark to swim faster. A shark's skin also **prevents** bacteria from growing on it, so scientists are copying this surface to design cleaner hospitals.

Velcro

burdock seeds

3 For NASA, protecting astronauts' eyes from the sun's rays is very important, but protecting their eyes from other dangerous radiation is also **essential**. Scientists studied how eagles and falcons clearly recognize their prey. Scientists discovered that the birds have yellow oil in their eyes, which filters out **harmful** radiation and allows them to see very clearly. NASA copied this oil, and it is now used by astronauts and pilots in Eagle Eyes® glasses. In addition to protecting eyes from dangerous rays, these sunglasses also improve vision in different weather conditions such as fog, sunlight, or just normal light.

4 To show how biomimicry could be used, Mercedes-Benz developed a concept car that was based on the shape of the tropical box-fish. Opinions were divided about the car's appearance, but the engineers at Mercedes-Benz chose to copy the boxfish skeleton to make their Bionic Car because of its strength and low weight. The boxfish's bony body protects the animal's insides from injury in the same way that a car needs to protect the people inside it. This shape also meant that the car had less air resistance and therefore used less fuel.

boxfish

Bionic Car

5 As these examples **illustrate**, biomimicry appears to have an **unlimited** number of applications. It will be interesting to see which problems nature helps us solve in the future.

WHILE READING

SKILLS

SCANNING TO FIND INFORMATION

Scanning means reading for specific information. When you scan a text, do not read every word. Look for key words that help you understand what the text is about and specific information. For example, look for names, numbers, pronouns, or groups of words related to the same topic/theme.

3 SCANNING TO FIND INFORMATION **Scan the article on pages 108–109 quickly to answer the questions.**

1 Which products are mentioned in the article?

____

____

2 Which plants or animals were copied to produce these products?

____

____

4 READING FOR MAIN IDEAS **Read the article. Choose the sentence that best summarizes the main idea of the article.**

a Though sharks can be dangerous, their skin is useful.

b In the future, nature can help us solve many important problems.

c Many useful products have been designed using biomimicry.

d Many useful discoveries have been made by accident.

5 ANNOTATING **Read the article again to find the answers to the questions. Annotate the text as you read. Look at page 74 for what to annotate. Write summary notes in the margin.**

1 Which two features of Velcro® make the strips stick together?

2 What are some uses of Velcro®?

3 What product mimics a shark's skin?

4 What does a shark's skin allow the shark to do?

5 Whose eyes did NASA want to protect from dangerous radiation?

6 What special feature of an eagle's eyes was copied to make sunglasses?

7 Which two features of a boxfish's skeleton make it good for engineers to copy?

8 What feature does the car copy that allows it to save fuel?

READING BETWEEN THE LINES

6 MAKING INFERENCES **Work with a partner. Discuss the questions.**

1 Why do you think Velcro® became popular with children's clothing companies?

2 Why do you think the Speedo Fastskin® swimsuit was controversial during the Beijing Olympics?

3 Why do people have different opinions about the Bionic Car?

CRITICAL THINKING

7 **Work with a partner. Discuss the questions.**

APPLY

What are the advantages of copying from nature?

ANALYZE

Do you think biomimicry will be more common in the future? Why or why not?

COLLABORATION

8 **A** Work in a small group. Imagine at least five products or inventions that could be inspired by nature. Think about:

- agriculture
- communication
- medicine
- architecture
- energy
- transportation

B Choose one item from your list. Find photos of the natural thing that inspired it, and answer the questions:

- What inspired your invention?
- How would your invention be similar to its inspiration? How would it be different?
- What would your invention look like?
- What purpose would it serve?

C Present a short report on your product or invention to the class.

kingfisher

bullet train

READING 2

PREPARING TO READ

1 UNDERSTANDING KEY VOCABULARY **You are going to read an article about technology in the future. Before you read the article, read the definitions below. Complete the sentences with the correct form of the words in bold.**

artificial (adj) not natural; made by people
break down (phr v) to stop working
electronic (adj) sent or accessed by means of a computer or other electronic device
movement (n) a change of position or place
object (n) a thing you can see or touch that isn't alive
personal (adj) belonging to or used by just one person
power (n) energy, usually electricity, used to provide heat, light, etc.
three-dimensional (adj) not flat; having depth, length, and width

1. When working on a computer, you should save your work often so that you don't lose your data if the ______________ fails.
2. Smartphones allow us to choose what we want to see and use. Each person's phone is very ______________ and doesn't look the same as anyone else's.
3. I don't need a paper ticket because I've got a(n) ______________ one on my phone.
4. ______________ imaging techniques give doctors a new way to view the inside of the human body.
5. The advances in technology for man-made arms and legs allow ______________ in all directions so people can continue to live a normal life.
6. Since cell phones were invented, it has been much easier for people to get help if their car ______________ on the highway.
7. Microscopes allow us to see ______________ that are too small to see with our eyes.
8. ______________ legs have become so advanced that people can use them to run marathons and climb mountains.

2 USING YOUR KNOWLEDGE **Work with a partner. Answer the questions.**

1 Do you think flying cars will be a reality someday? Why or why not?

____

____

2 What is a 3D printer? What is it used for?

____

____

3 How can robots help people who are missing arms or legs?

____

____

TECHNOLOGY OF THE FUTURE

❶ What will the world of the future be like? Will it be easier or more difficult? Many people are confident that technology is going to help solve some of the most challenging problems we have on Earth today. Other people are worried that new technology may solve old problems but create new ones. Here are three predictions about the world of tomorrow.

Flying Cars

❷ When we dream about the future, many of us like to think that we will be able to exit our garages and take to the skies in our own **personal** flying car. The advantages are obvious. This technology would allow **three-dimensional** freedom of **movement**. We could fly at 300 miles (480 kilometers) per hour, avoiding traffic lights, busy roads, and speeding tickets. However, some people point to the disadvantages of flying cars. They claim that there are certain to be problems with traffic control. If the cars become popular, there is likely to be a problem with air traffic congestion. Another big problem is mechanical failure. What will happen if the cars **break down**? These are problems we must expect if flying cars become a reality.

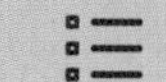

3D Printers

❸ We have all printed out **electronic** documents on paper, and most of us are probably aware of 3D printing, a process by which three-dimensional **objects** are created. 3D printers build an object using layers of liquid plastic, metal, or other materials. They build up the layers line by line like a normal printer until the object is complete. Car companies like BMW and Volkswagen already use 3D printers to make life-size models of car parts, and medical technology companies have already used 3D printing to make body parts, such as **artificial** ears. Some people even print their own small objects, such as jewelry and toys, with 3D printers. But did you know that 3D printing can create something as large as a house, or that experiments are being conducted into printing biological tissue? Before long, it might be possible to use 3D printing to create affordable housing, print organs for medical transplants, or even print food.

Robot Suits

❹ Finally, imagine having your own Ironman suit. Several companies are trying to build a practical robot "exoskeleton." This is a suit of robot arms and legs that follows the wearer's movements. It will allow the wearer to lift heavy objects, walk long distances, and even punch through walls! There are obvious military advantages for this technology, but there are also benefits for people with disabilities. The suit might help people walk again after disease or injury. However, the obvious disadvantage at the moment is cost. Even a simple exoskeleton can cost hundreds of thousands of dollars. Another problem is battery life. A suit like this needs a lot of **power**; at the moment, the batteries last only about 15 minutes. One other problem is that a badly programed robot suit could injure the wearer. You wouldn't want your robot leg or arm bending the wrong way, for instance.

❺ In the future, although we might be able to fly to work, print out a new pair of shoes, or lift a car above our heads, there are plenty of problems to solve before all of this will be possible. In the meantime, we can dream!

WHILE READING

SKILLS

USING A T-CHART

A T-chart is a kind of graphic organizer. It is useful for examining two sides or aspects of a topic, such as advantages/disadvantages or pros/cons.

3 TAKING NOTES **Read the article on pages 114–115 and complete the T-charts.**

flying car	
advantages	disadvantages

3D printing	
advantages	disadvantages

robot suit	
advantages	disadvantages

4 READING FOR DETAILS **Read the article again and write *T* (true), *F* (false), or *DNS* (does not say) next to the statements. Then correct the false statements.**

_______ 1 Flying cars will allow us to avoid traffic congestion on the roads.

_______ 2 Mechanical failure will not be a problem for flying cars.

_______ 3 We might be able to print things like necklaces or chairs in the future.

_______ 4 3D printing was invented in 1984.

_______ 5 BMW and Volkswagen are going to use 3D printing soon.

_______ 6 Robot suits are heavy objects.

_______ 7 The battery life of a robot suit is short at the moment.

READING BETWEEN THE LINES

5 MAKING INFERENCES **Work with a partner. Answer the questions.**

1 Why is mechanical failure a possible problem in a flying car?

____

2 Why will flying cars cause traffic congestion instead of reducing it?

____

3 What do you think could be the benefits of robot suits?

____

4 Why wouldn't you want a robot suit arm to bend the wrong way?

____

CRITICAL THINKING

6 SYNTHESIZING **Work with a partner. Imagine the year is 2030. Use ideas from Reading 1 and Reading 2 to discuss the questions.**

APPLY

Which inventions do you think you will use regularly? Why?

EVALUATE

Which inventions are no longer used because something better has replaced them?

EVALUATE

Which inventions failed because they had too many problems?

COLLABORATION

7 **A** Work in a small group. Research another technology that may become more popular in the future. Make notes on the following questions and anything else that you find interesting:

- Who will use the technology?
- How will it benefit people?
- Will it help the environment? How?
- What are its disadvantages?
- How soon might we be using the technology?

B Present the technology to the class. Then vote on which technology:

- is the most exciting
- is most likely to help the environment
- is most likely to make life easier
- has the greatest risk

LANGUAGE DEVELOPMENT

MAKING PREDICTIONS WITH MODALS AND ADVERBS OF CERTAINTY

LANGUAGE

Use *will, could,* and *won't* with an adverb of certainty before the main verb to talk about future predictions. For example:

100% = *will definitely*

Cars **will definitely** become more efficient in the future.

90% = *will probably*

The next generation **will probably** use more digital devices.

50% = *could possibly*

We **could possibly** see humans walking on Mars soon.

20% = *probably won't*

We **probably won't** have flying cars.

0% = *definitely won't*

We **definitely won't** be traveling to other stars.

1 Complete the sentences about the future using modal and adverb phrases with the meaning in parentheses.

1 In years to come, biofuels ____________ become more important. (100%)
2 Genetic modification ____________ be very controversial before the end of the decade. (30%)
3 In the near future, electronic human implants ____________ become very common. (90%)
4 Biomimicry ____________ be a growing industry before too long. (90%)
5 Robotic cars ____________ be everyday products within the next ten years. (100%)
6 Everyone ____________ own a personal Ironman suit within two years. (0%)
7 By 2025, many people ____________ have a 3D printer in their homes. (50%)

2 Look again at Exercise 1 and underline the phrases that refer to future time.

PREFIXES

LANGUAGE

Prefixes are added to the beginning of a word to make a new word with a different meaning. Understanding the meaning of prefixes can help you guess the general meaning of difficult academic or technical words.

3 **Look at these prefixes, their meanings, and the examples. Add your own examples to the chart.**

prefix	meaning	example
de-	reverse or go down	decrease, ________ , ________
dis-	reverse or opposite	disagree, ________ , ________
en-	cause	enable, ________ , ________
pre-	before	prevent, ________ , ________
re-	again	rebuild, ________ , ________
trans-	across, through	transportation, ________ , ________
un-	remove, reverse, not	unlikely, ________ , ________

4 **Compare the pairs of sentences. Use the chart above and write whether the sentences have the *same* or *opposite* meanings.**

1 Flying cars are **unsafe**.
Flying cars are dangerous. ________

2 We have to **rethink** the way we use technology.
We have to think again about how we use technology. ________

3 Genetic engineering **dehumanizes** us.
Genetic engineering makes us more human. ________

4 Can this software **translate** a document from French to English?
Can this software change the language of a document from French to English? ________

5 Seat belts in cars **prevent** many injuries and deaths.
Seat belts cause many injuries and deaths. ________

6 This laboratory is very **disorganized**.
This laboratory is neat. ________

7 The typesize on your presentation is too small. Can you **enlarge** it?
Can you make it bigger? ________

5 **Work with a partner. Choose words from the chart above and make five predictions about new technology.**

WATCH AND LISTEN

GLOSSARY

canal (n) a man-made river built for boats to travel along or to take water where it is needed

frame (n) the basic structure of a building, vehicle, piece of furniture, etc. that other parts are added onto

concrete (n) a hard substance that is used in building and made by mixing sand, water, small stones, and cement

crane (n) a large, usually tall machine used for lifting and moving heavy things

pump (n) a piece of equipment that pushes liquid or gas somewhere, especially through pipes or tubes

PREPARING TO WATCH

1 ACTIVATING YOUR KNOWLEDGE **You are going to watch a video about a river in China. Before you watch, work with a partner and discuss the questions.**

1 What are some inventions to help us control our natural environment?

2 How does water get into your home?

3 How does water become clean enough to drink?

2 PREDICTING CONTENT USING VISUALS **Work with a partner. Look at the photos from the video and discuss the questions.**

1 What do you think these people are building?

2 What problem could this project solve?

WHILE WATCHING

3 UNDERSTANDING MAIN IDEAS **Watch the video. Answer the questions.**

1 Where do most of the people in China live? ______________________

2 What problem does China have? ______________________

3 How is each section of the canal built? ______________________

4 Why does the crane operator have to be very careful?

____

5 When will the project be completed? _______________

6 Who will the new canal help? _______________

4 UNDERSTANDING DETAILS **Watch the video again. Correct the student notes.**

1 Problem = people in north need food
2 Solution = build a lake
3 Length = 570 miles
4 Weight of each concrete section = 12 tons
5 End of each section = 1 meter higher than other end
6 Finish date = 2020

CRITICAL THINKING

5 **Work in a small group. Discuss the questions.**

APPLY

What are the five most important inventions in the past 100 years?

ANALYZE

What is the purpose, along with some positive and negative effects, of each invention?

EVALUATE

Which invention has positively affected the most people?

COLLABORATION

6 **A** Work in a small group. Discuss the aqueduct project from the video. Make a list of three possible advantages and three possible disadvantages of the project. Think about:

- people
- quality of life
- money
- environment
- sustainability

B Compare your lists with the class. Do the advantages of the project outweigh the disadvantages? Decide the answer as a class.

FASHION

LEARNING OBJECTIVES

Key Reading Skill	Distinguishing fact from opinion
Additional Reading Skills	Understanding key vocabulary; using your knowledge; reading for main ideas; reading for details; making inferences; skimming; scanning to find information; taking notes; synthesizing
Language Development	Vocabulary for the fashion business

ACTIVATE YOUR KNOWLEDGE

Work with a partner. Discuss the questions.

1 Which clothing companies are popular in your country? Why are they popular?

2 Why do people buy designer clothing?

3 Do you prefer designer clothing or clothes that are not designer? Why or why not?

4 Are stores that sell cheap clothes popular in your country?

PREPARING TO READ

1 UNDERSTANDING KEY VOCABULARY **You are going to read an article about fashion. Read the sentences. Complete the definitions with the correct form of the words in bold.**

1. When you shop for clothes, do you search for specific **brands**, or do you just buy what you like?
2. When a clothing company raises its prices, it is not unusual for the company's sales **volume** to fall.
3. Everyone was talking about the new designer **collections** at the spring fashion show in Milan.
4. My favorite store just launched their new coats for the fall **season**.
5. **Cotton** clothes are cool and soft, but they wrinkle easily.
6. These days, many clothing companies **manufacture** their clothes in Vietnam, Cambodia, or other countries in Southeast Asia.
7. New companies have to **invest** millions of dollars in building factories and training employees.

a ______________ (n) a time of year when particular things happen

b ______________ (v) to make goods in a large quantity in a factory

c ______________ (n) amount of something, especially when it is large

d ______________ (n) a group of new clothes produced by a fashion house

e ______________ (n) a plant with white fibers used for making cloth

f ______________ (v) to use money for the purpose of making a profit, for example, by building a factory

g ______________ (n) the name of a product or group of products made by a company

2 USING YOUR KNOWLEDGE **Work with a partner. Answer the questions.**

1 What does the term *fast fashion* mean to you?

____

____

2 How often do fashions usually change? Explain your answer.

____

____

3 If fashion designers changed fashions every month, what effect would this have on shoppers? On the clothing industry?

____

____

3 **After you read the article on pages 126–127, check your answers to Exercise 2.**

IS *FAST FASHION* TAKING OVER?

1 The fashion industry has changed significantly in recent years. Traditionally, fashion retailers[1] created two clothing **collections** per year, called **seasons**. Each season was a collection of clothes for spring/summer and fall/winter. Nowadays, in contrast, they can design and **manufacture** clothes in as little as four weeks. *Fast fashion* means that the latest designs shown at the fashion shows in Paris, London, New York, and Milan can be copied and sold in shopping malls within a month. A typical fast-fashion retailer can stock 10,000 designs annually, compared with 2,000 for its high-fashion competitors. The largest fast-fashion retailers have annual sales in the billions of dollars.

2 The advantages of rapidly changing fashions are clear. Shortening the life cycle of a product means that if a design doesn't sell well within a week, it is taken out of the stores and replaced with a new one. This is good for manufacturers, as it means a greater **volume** of sales. It is also good for customers, who can keep up with fast-moving trends cheaply and who can enjoy finding something new every time they visit the store.

3 However, there are also a number of disadvantages to the fast-fashion approach. Perhaps the biggest concern is the impact of wasted clothes on the environment. The low cost of most fast fashion enables shoppers to buy several new sets of clothes each season instead of wearing the same outfits year after year. This means that huge amounts of clothing are thrown away. Furthermore, with fashions changing so quickly, **cotton** growers need to produce more cotton more cheaply, and that means using more pesticides and chemicals. A third problem is the theft of ideas. Fashion houses **invest** a lot of time and money in new designs, only to see these ideas stolen and copied by fast-fashion companies.

4 Fast fashion rests at one end of the fashion scale. At the other end is high-end designer clothing, where major changes are also happening. At the same time as fast fashion is becoming more and more popular, wealthy consumers worldwide are buying more and more expensive, luxury **brands**. Many well-off customers buy designer clothes just to show that they can afford them, but others choose luxury brands for their quality, saying that they will last longer. They have a point. Due to their longer lifespan, expensive designer clothes are more environmentally friendly.

5 In short, these days it seems that the fashion industry is changing almost as fast as the fashion it produces—but what do you think? We would like to hear your comments about the fashion industry today.

[1]**retailer** (n) someone who sells products to people

COMMENTS
6 comments

Carmen
I'd love to have the money to buy designer clothes, but I have to buy cheaper products because I don't have much money. I'm sure the quality is not as good as clothes with designer labels.
Like 14 Reply

Ahmet
Designer fashion is a waste of money. Wearing brand names is just free advertising for that company, and I don't think the quality is any different.
Like 13 Reply

Jasmine
Great article!
I love fast fashion! I enjoy looking good and having lots of clothes. Fast fashion allows me to buy lots of clothes really cheaply. Why should I feel bad about throwing away cheap clothes when they go out of fashion? I can just go out and get more.
Like 0 Reply

Ben
Response to Jasmine
People like you make me really angry. That is such a selfish attitude. Think about the environment. Don't you care about wasting all those clothes? At least donate the clothes to charity if you don't want them anymore.
Like 7 Reply

Sara
Style is important to me. I study fashion at college and I would never buy fast fashion. I don't want to look like everyone else. I prefer to buy secondhand clothes because older clothes were designed to last. I have my own style. I don't need to copy Paris or Milan.
Like 11 Reply

Fatima
I can understand why people like fast fashion, but I prefer to pay for quality, and if the store has ethically produced clothes, then that is perfect. I agree with Ben: we need to take care of the planet; otherwise, our children won't have a planet to live on. I would rather pay more and know I'm helping to protect the Earth.
Like 31 Reply

WHILE READING

4 READING FOR MAIN IDEAS **Read the article on pages 126–127, and number the main ideas in the order that they are mentioned. Not all the ideas are mentioned. Remember to annotate the article as you read.**

a designer clothing ______
b advantages of fast fashion __1__
c fast fashion shows ______
d the definition of fast fashion ______
e disadvantages of fast fashion ______

5 READING FOR DETAILS **Look at the article again and correct the factual mistakes in the sentences. The first one has been done for you as an example.**

1 Traditional fashion retailers annually produce 10,000 designs.
Traditional fashion retailers annually produce 2,000 designs.

2 High-end fashion designs that are unpopular are withdrawn in less than a month.
____

3 Traditional fashion is good for the manufacturer because of the greater volume of sales.
____

4 The biggest problem with fast fashion is the theft of ideas.
____

5 Cotton growers need to produce more, so they have to use less fertilizer.
____

6 Designer clothing is popular with middle-class shoppers.
____

READING BETWEEN THE LINES

6 MAKING INFERENCES **Look at the comments about the article and answer the questions.**

1 Who is against designer fashion?

____

2 Who would like to buy more expensive clothes?

____

3 Who doesn't like to follow fashion trends?

____

4 Who has the most likes? Why?

____

5 Who has the fewest likes? Why?

____

CRITICAL THINKING

7 **Work with a partner. Discuss the questions.**

APPLY

Which comment from the reading do you agree with the most? Why?

APPLY

Do you shop at fast-fashion stores? How often? What do you buy?

ANALYZE

Is fashion more important to younger or older people? Why?

COLLABORATION

8 **A** Work in a small group. Reading 1 mentions some ways in which the fashion industry is bad for the environment. Research other ways that the fashion industry is harmful. Make a list of the five effects that you think are the most harmful.

B Compare lists as a class. Brainstorm alternatives to fast fashion, such as buying secondhand clothes. Assign one student to write the ideas on the board. Then vote on the top three alternatives.

READING 2

PREPARING TO READ

1 UNDERSTANDING KEY VOCABULARY **Read the definitions. Complete the sentences with the correct form of the words in bold.**

conditions (n) the physical environment where people live or work

import (v) to buy a product from another country and bring it into your country

multinational (adj) referring to a business or company that has offices, stores, or factories in several countries

offshore (adj) located in another country

outsource (v) to have work done by another company, often in another country, rather than in your own company

textile (n) cloth or fabric that is made by crossing threads under and over each other

wage (n) money that people earn for working

1. Some ______________ companies are so big that they have branches in more than a hundred countries.
2. Designers at famous fashion houses can earn high ______________ .
3. The workers at that factory are well-paid, and their working ______________ are safe and comfortable.
4. Scotland is famous for producing beautiful wool ______________, which are often used to make a skirt for men called a kilt.
5. At one time, the company made all its products in the United States. In recent years, however, it decided to ______________ its production to Singapore.
6. Many manufacturers do large parts of their production in ______________ factories because materials and labor are cheaper in other countries.
7. We ______________ fabric from China, then we sew and finish the shirts here.

2 USING YOUR KNOWLEDGE **Answer the questions. Then discuss your answers with a partner.**

1 Why do some companies outsource their production to other countries?

____

____

2 What are the benefits for a country when a multinational company moves its production there?

____

____

3 Are there any disadvantages for workers when multinational companies base their factories in their countries?

____

____

3 SKIMMING **Skim the title and the first paragraph of the essay on pages 132–133.**

1 What is the essay about?

____

____

2 What is the writer's point of view about this? How do you know?

____

____

OFFSHORE TEXTILE PRODUCTION: WHY IT MUST CHANGE

1 The world's consumption of fashion is huge. To give just one example, the United States alone **imported** more than 126 billion dollars' worth of **textiles** in 2015. As consumption has risen, prices have fallen. Today, a hand-finished shirt may cost as little as five dollars. To make clothes at these low prices, companies have to keep costs down. They use **offshore** production to do this. Large **multinational** companies **outsource** their production to developing countries like Egypt or Cambodia, where workers are paid much less than in developed countries. Supporters of outsourcing claim that it helps local economies, but I believe it is harmful for two main reasons.

2 First, overseas workers usually receive very low **wages**. These workers, many of them women and children, often work 14 hours a day and earn less than a hundred dollars a month. One study of 15 countries found that textile workers earned less than 40% of the money they needed to live on each month. In some countries this figure is even lower. Also, most workers are paid by the piece. This means they might earn only a few cents for making a dress that sells for hundreds of dollars in the United States or Europe. Such low wages are wrong and unfair. As Priya Kapoor, a human rights researcher in Delhi, says, "Garment workers in countries like India and Bangladesh can't afford to pay their basic needs like food and healthcare. We need to establish a fair wage for the work they do."

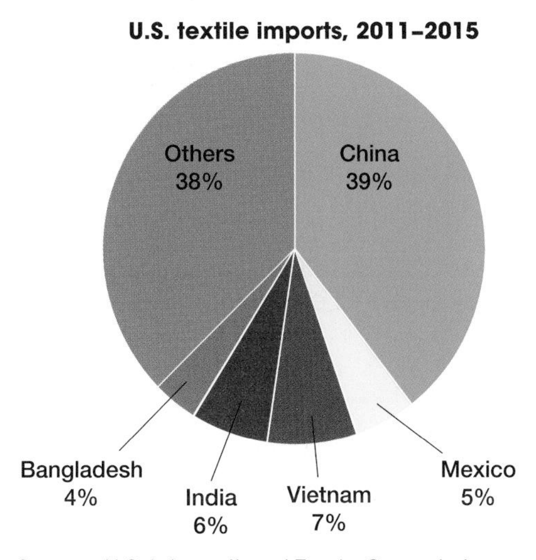

Source: U.S. International Trade Commission

3 The second problem with outsourcing is that working **conditions** in many offshore factories are uncomfortable and unsafe. It is a fact that worker protection laws like those in developed nations either don't exist or often are not followed. As a result, workers are exposed to chemicals, dust, and unsafe levels of noise from sewing machines. I saw this myself when I visited a clothing factory in Bangladesh in 2015. The noise was so loud that I had to cover my ears. Moreover, factory buildings are often unsafe, and horrible accidents happen. For example, the whole world was shocked in 2012 when a fire broke out at a garment factory in Dhaka, Bangladesh, that killed 117 people and injured 200.

4 I realize some experts, like the economist David Schneider, say that outsourcing benefits local economies by providing jobs at higher wages than local workers can make by working in agriculture. Supporters of outsourcing point out that people in developing countries often line up to take jobs in multinational factories. These arguments may be correct, but in my opinion they do not justify the low wages and dangerous conditions found in many overseas factories today. If multinationals are going to continue to benefit from low production costs by using overseas suppliers, I believe they should contribute a much larger share of their massive profits to correcting these problems and improving social conditions in the countries where they are located—starting today.

WHILE READING

4 SCANNING TO FIND INFORMATION **Complete the sentences with words from the essay.**

1 ______________ companies outsource their factories to countries where workers are paid less than they are in developed countries.

2 One study found that workers in offshore factories earned only ______________ percent of the money they needed each month, even though they worked 14 hours a day.

3 In developing countries, worker-protection laws often ______________ .

4 ______________ people died in the Dhaka fire in 2012.

5 David Schneider is a(n) ______________ .

5 TAKING NOTES **Complete the chart with the writer's reasons, evidence, and conclusion. You do not need to write complete sentences.**

main argument: Outsourcing is harmful for 2 reasons.

reason 1: ______________	reason 2: ______________
evidence:	evidence:
(1) ______________	(5) ______________
(2) ______________	(6) ______________
(3) ______________	(7) ______________
(4) ______________	(8) ______________
	(9) ______________

conclusion: ______________

READING BETWEEN THE LINES

SKILLS

DISTINGUISHING FACT FROM OPINION

When you read a text, you need to be able to decide which points are facts and which points are opinions. A *fact* is a true statement that can be proven. An *opinion* usually expresses a person's idea, judgment, or position. Academic writers use facts and reasons to support their opinions and make them sound convincing.

6 DISTINGUISHING FACT FROM OPINION **Look at the sentences from Reading 2. Write *F* (fact) or *O* (opinion) next to each sentence. Compare your answers with a partner.**

1 … the United States alone imported more than 126 billion dollars' worth of textiles in 2015. ________
2 Supporters of outsourcing claim that it helps local economies, but I believe it is harmful for two main reasons. ________
3 … most workers are paid by the piece. This means they might earn only a few cents for making a dress that sells for hundreds of dollars in the United States or Europe. ________
4 … worker-protection laws like those in developed nations either don't exist or often are not followed. ________
5 … working conditions in many offshore factories are uncomfortable and unsafe. ________
6 These arguments may be correct, but in my opinion they do not justify the low wages and dangerous conditions found in many overseas factories today. ________

CRITICAL THINKING

7 SYNTHESIZING **Work with a partner. Use ideas from Reading 1 and Reading 2 to answer the questions.**

APPLY

Do you agree or disagree with the opinions in Exercise 6? Explain your reasons.

EVALUATE

Should multinationals that outsource their factories do more for the local community? If so, what?

COLLABORATION

8 **A** Work in two groups. Prepare arguments for a class debate.

- Group A: Prepare arguments for overseas production of clothing. Include arguments against those in Reading 2, and add your own arguments.
- Group B: Prepare arguments against overseas production of clothing. Add at least three arguments to those in Reading 2.

B Have a debate. Your teacher will moderate and decide the winner.

LANGUAGE DEVELOPMENT

VOCABULARY FOR THE FASHION BUSINESS

Read the sentences. Complete the definitions on page 137 with the correct form of the words in bold.

1 One of the biggest costs for retailers is **advertising**, but without it, customers have no way of getting information about stores and products.

2 Smart **consumers** shop for clothes during the off-season. For example, they buy winter coats in the spring.

3 Some shoppers only buy clothes made by **designer labels**. If it's not Gucci® or Prada®, they are not interested.

4 In the United States, Forever 21® and H&M® are **competitors**. They have similar prices and they try to attract similar customers.

5 In the clothing business, very little **manufacturing** is done in the United States. Most companies have their factories in other countries.

6 China and India are the two biggest **suppliers** of cotton in the world. Every big clothing company buys from them.

7 In some countries, workers are paid only 14 cents an hour for their **labor**.

8 As well as clothing companies, computer companies also find it cheaper to make their products **overseas**, mainly in Asia.

a ______________________ (n) a person or company that sells a product or service

b ______________________ (n) a company that makes or designs expensive clothes

c ______________________ (adv) in, from or to a country located across the ocean

d ______________________ (n) a person who buys things to use

e ______________________ (n) the business of creating or sending out announcements in magazines, on television, etc. to attract shoppers

f ______________________ (n) businesses that try to win or do better than other businesses selling almost the same products

g ______________________ (n) work

h ______________________ (n) the process of making things, especially in a factory

WATCH AND LISTEN

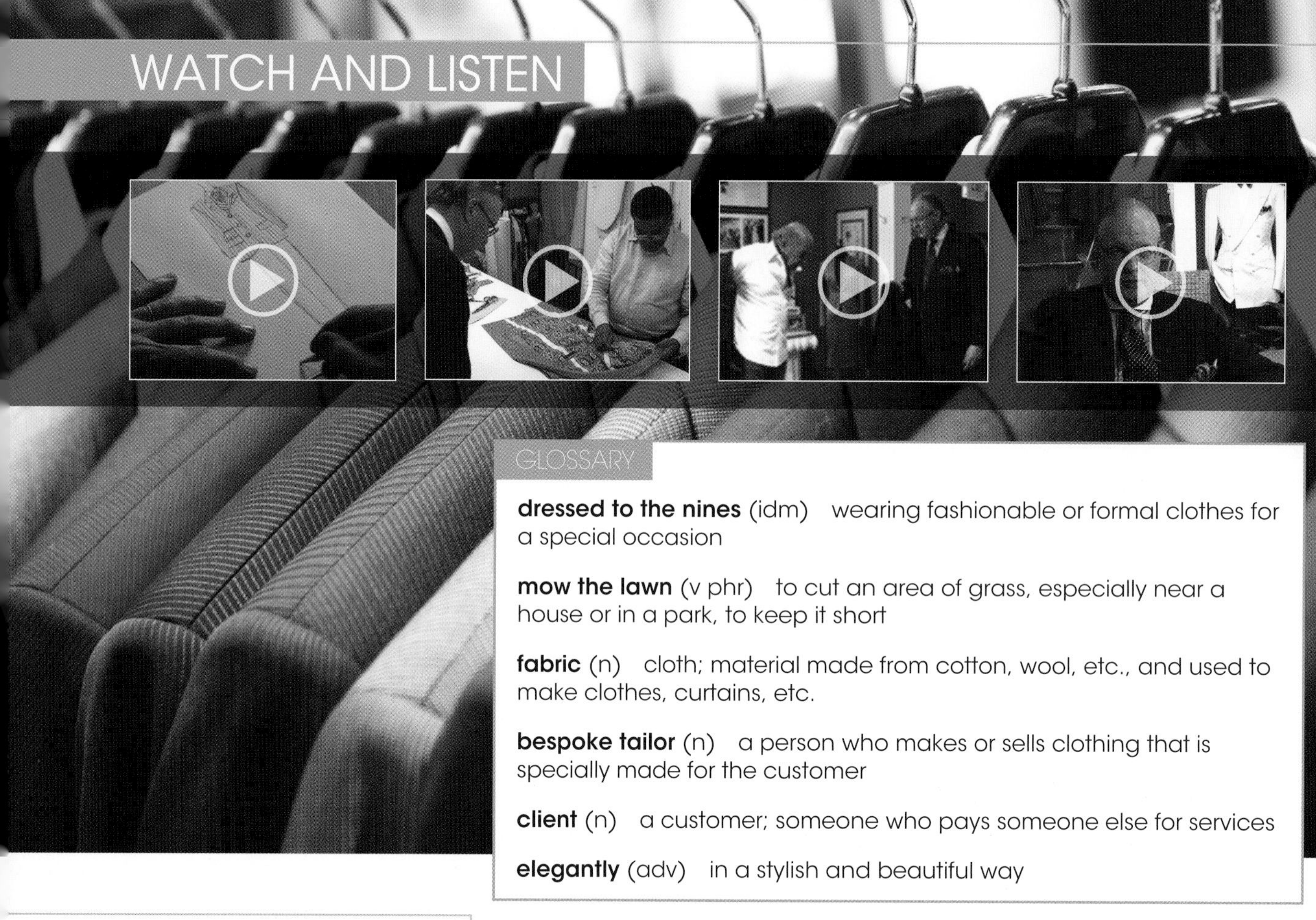

GLOSSARY

dressed to the nines (idm) wearing fashionable or formal clothes for a special occasion

mow the lawn (v phr) to cut an area of grass, especially near a house or in a park, to keep it short

fabric (n) cloth; material made from cotton, wool, etc., and used to make clothes, curtains, etc.

bespoke tailor (n) a person who makes or sells clothing that is specially made for the customer

client (n) a customer; someone who pays someone else for services

elegantly (adv) in a stylish and beautiful way

PREPARING TO WATCH

1 ACTIVATING YOUR KNOWLEDGE **Work with a partner. Discuss the questions.**

1 Look at the clothes you have on. Where were they made? Who do you think made them?

2 Describe formal clothes for men and women in your country.

3 If you could have one item of clothing specially made just for you, what would that be?

2 PREDICTING CONTENT USING VISUALS **Work with a partner. Look at the photos from the video and discuss the questions.**

1 What industry do you think the men work in?

2 Do you think these clothes are made by machine or by hand?

3 Where would people wear clothes like these?

WHILE WATCHING

3 UNDERSTANDING MAIN IDEAS **Watch the video. Number the events in order (1–6).**

a father and son talk ______

b man signs his name on drawing of a suit ______

c two men look at the inside of a jacket ______
d man cuts material with scissors ______
e man puts on black jacket ______
f man looks closely at the material of a jacket ______

4 UNDERSTANDING DETAILS **Watch the video again. Check the clothes you see.**

1 ☐ hat
2 ☐ jacket
3 ☐ pants
4 ☐ shirt
5 ☐ shoes
6 ☐ sweater
7 ☐ tie
8 ☐ winter coat

5 MAKING INFERENCES **Work with a partner. Discuss the questions and give reasons for your answers.**

1 Does the designer prefer formal or informal clothes?
2 Do you think his company makes a large number of jackets each year?
3 How do you think the speaker feels about the way many young people dress today?
4 What does the speaker mean when he says that he wants his clients to step out of their comfort zone?

CRITICAL THINKING

6 Work with a partner. Discuss your answers.

APPLY

When do you wear formal clothes? Do you feel or act differently when you are wearing them?

EVALUATE

Do you own any handmade items? Are they better than items made by machines? Why or why not?

COLLABORATION

7 **A** Work in a small group. Compare fast fashion and tailor-made clothing. Make a list of five advantages and five disadvantages of each type of fashion. How might it be possible to produce clothing in a way that combines some of the advantages of each method without the disadvantages? Take notes on your ideas.

B Present your best idea to the class. Vote on the most successful idea as a class.

UNIT 8

ECONOMICS

LEARNING OBJECTIVES

Key Reading Skills	Skimming; understanding line graphs
Additional Reading Skills	Understanding key vocabulary; using your knowledge; reading for main ideas; reading for details; making inferences; scanning to find information; annotating; taking notes; synthesizing
Language Development	Nouns and adjectives for economics; nouns for economic trends

ACTIVATE YOUR KNOWLEDGE

Work with a partner. Discuss the questions.

1. Do you believe it is important for people to be informed about economics? Why or why not?
2. What causes some countries to be rich and other countries to be poor?
3. How has the economy of your country changed in recent years?

READING 1

PREPARING TO READ

1 UNDERSTANDING KEY VOCABULARY **You are going to read an article about investments. Read the sentences. Complete the definitions with the correct form of the words in bold.**

1. During the **recession** of 2007–2009, people all over the world lost their jobs and were forced to sell their homes.
2. At my bank, the **interest rate** on a loan to buy a car is about 4.5%.
3. Since Apple Computer company **stocks and shares** went on sale in 1976, their value has increased by more than 28,000%.
4. Real estate, that is, land or buildings, is an excellent **investment** in large cities like Los Angeles or Tokyo.
5. My father is a careful **investor**. He buys assets, like buildings and classic cars, that increase slowly but surely over time.
6. After a natural disaster such as a tsunami or fire, the homes and businesses in an area usually go down in **value**.
7. If you buy gold, you can probably expect to get a high rate of **return** on your investment.

a ______________ (n) the percentage amount that you pay when you borrow money, or receive when you lend money, for a period of time

b ______________ (n) profit on an investment

c ______________ (n) parts of a publicly owned business that can be bought and sold as investments

d ______________ (n) someone who puts money in a bank, business, etc. to make a profit

e ______________ (n) how much money something could be sold for

f ______________ (n) a period when the economy of a country is not doing well, but not as bad as a depression

g ______________ (n) something such as stocks, bonds, or property that you buy in order to make a profit

2 USING YOUR KNOWLEDGE **Work with a partner. Answer the questions.**

1 If people want to make money, what can they invest in?

____

____

2 What is the safest investment, in your opinion? Explain.

____

____

3 Do you think it is better to invest in gold or in classic cars? Explain your reasons.

____

____

Singapore is one of the world's leading financial centers.

INVESTING: TWO ALTERNATIVES TO CONSIDER

1 In a **recession**, **interest rates** are low. This means that keeping your money in a bank may not be the best way of making money. **Stocks and shares** are also risky when the economy takes a dive[1]. So where should you invest to make the most of your money? For the brave **investor**, there are a range of alternative **investments**. Gold and classic cars are two popular investments because their market **value** tends to go up with time.

Gold

2 Over time, gold has been a very good investment, though the price has fluctuated[2] in recent years, as the graph here shows. From about $283 an ounce at the turn of the 21st century, the price had more than doubled by 2006 and then doubled again, to $1,224, by 2010. Continuing the upward trend, the price rose sharply in 2011 and then reached a peak of $1,800 an ounce in 2012. However, by the end of 2015 the price had fallen dramatically, to $1,160. Forecasters expect the price to stay in this range through 2020, so if you are thinking about investing in gold, you may want to consider one famous investor's advice. Warren Buffet, one of the richest men in the world, dislikes gold as an investment. He points out that historically, the stock market has brought in significantly higher **returns** than gold. This is not always true, however. Between 2000 and 2012, for example, gold performed nearly ten times better than the stock market.

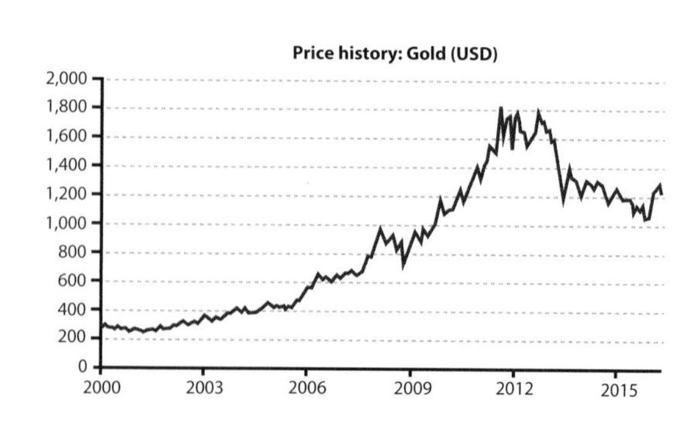

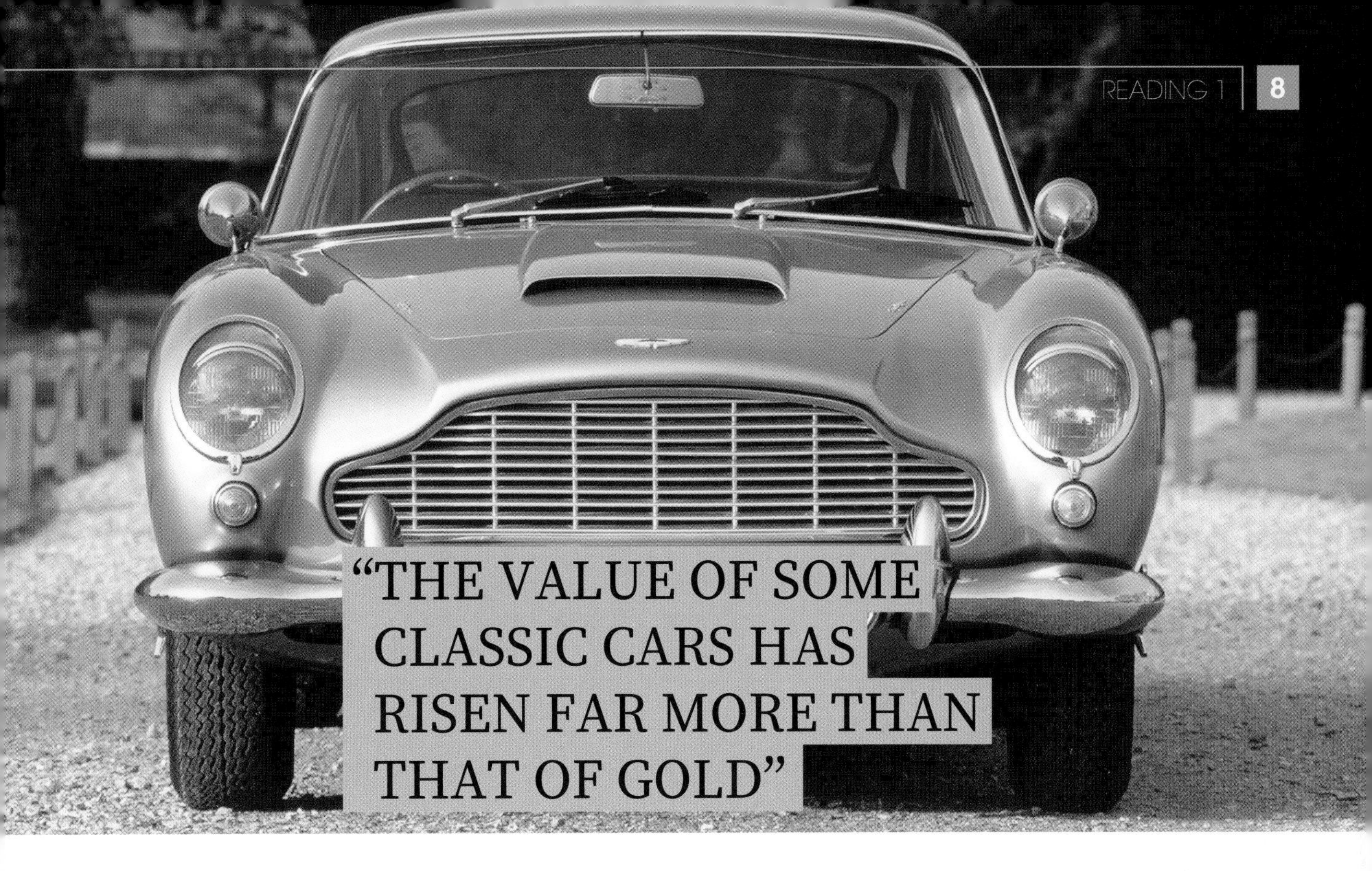

Classic Cars

3 While gold and stocks are both excellent investment options, some people prefer investments that they can use and enjoy. For these people, classic cars are one way to have fun and make lots of money. In fact, over the last 30 or 40 years, the value of some classic cars has risen far more than that of gold or other investments like houses. As an example, a 1972 Ferrari Dino 246 GT cost around $13,000 in 1980 but is worth as much as $450,000 now. A 1955 Mercedes Benz 300SL cost about $36,000 in 1980 but is worth more than $1 million now. But neither of these cars compares to what is perhaps the best investment ever: A man in Tennessee bought the Aston Martin DB5 that was used in two of the James Bond films. This car cost just $7,000 in 1980 but sold in 2010 for an incredible $4.1 million! That is more than 20 times the price of an average American home!

4 In sum, the prospect of making lots of money through investing is very exciting, but one must never forget that investing is a risky business. Gold prices rise, but they also fall. Classic cars need to be kept in excellent condition to increase in value and, because fashions change, investors have to guess which car to invest in. If you are smart and lucky, you may make a big profit—but remember, there are no guarantees.

[1]**take a dive** (v) If a value or price takes a dive, it suddenly becomes less.

[2]**fluctuate** (v) to keep changing, especially in level or amount

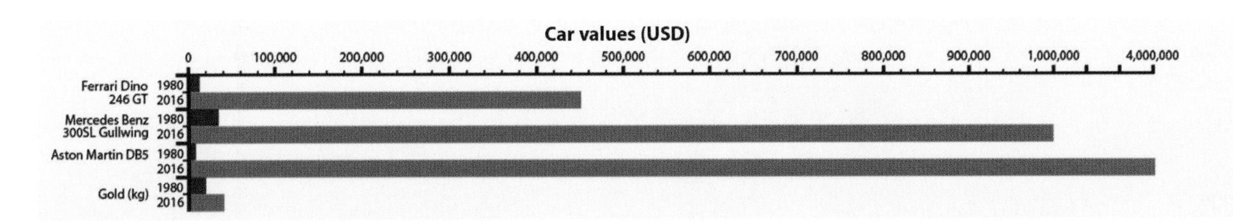

WHILE READING

SKILLS

SKIMMING

To skim a text, read it quickly to get a general idea of what it is about. Don't read every word. It is enough to read the title, the introductory paragraph, the concluding paragraph, and perhaps the first sentence of each main body paragraph. It is also useful to look at any photos or diagrams in the text.

3 SKIMMING **Skim the article and the graphs on pages 144–145. Check the topics that the article discusses.**

- ☐ causes of a recession
- ☐ two popular investments
- ☐ the price of gold over time
- ☐ the stock market in 2016
- ☐ classic cars as an investment
- ☐ the risks of investing

4 READING FOR MAIN IDEAS **Look at your answers to Exercise 3. Find the main ideas and write them in the order that they appear in the reading.**

Paragraph 1 ______

Paragraph 2 ______

Paragraph 3 ______

Paragraph 4 ______

5 READING FOR DETAILS **Read the article. Answer the questions using a figure from the article. Remember to annotate the text as you read.**

1. Approximately how much did gold cost per ounce at the beginning of the 21st century? ______
2. What happened to the price of gold in 2006? ______
3. In which year was the price of gold the highest? How much did it cost per ounce? ______
4. According to forecasters, what will happen to the price of gold between now and 2020? ______
5. How much did a Ferrari Dino 246 GT cost in 1980? ______
6. What is a 1955 Mercedes Benz 300SL worth now? ______
7. How much did the Aston Martin used in the James Bond films sell for in 2010? ______

READING BETWEEN THE LINES

6 MAKING INFERENCES **Work with a partner. Discuss the questions.**

1 If you followed Warren Buffet's advice, would you invest in the stock market or in gold? Why?

2 Which investment had a better return in the first part of the 21st century: gold or a classic car?

3 Are classic cars a risky investment? Why or why not?

CRITICAL THINKING

7 **Work with a partner. Discuss the questions.**

APPLY
What kind of investments do you or your family make?

ANALYZE
If you could afford to buy the James Bond Aston Martin, would you? Explain your reasons.

ANALYZE
Why do you think the writer of Reading 1 says that gold and classic cars are options for "the brave investor"?

EVALUATE
Are there any investments that you definitely would not make? Why not?

COLLABORATION

8 **A** Work with a partner. Imagine that you have $1 million to invest. How would you invest the money? Discuss the benefits and risks of each of the following types of investment. Then choose two or more places to invest your money.

- stocks and bonds
- gold
- classic cars
- real estate
- art
- a savings account
- a business startup
- rare coins

B Share your investment choices and reasons with another pair. Repeat with at least two more pairs.

C Choose one type of investment. Prepare a 30-second marketing "pitch" with your partner, and present it to the class.

READING 2

PREPARING TO READ

1 UNDERSTANDING KEY VOCABULARY **You are going to read an article about income and expenditure. Before you read the article, read the sentences below. Complete the definitions with the correct form of the words in bold.**

1 My family has a comfortable **standard of living**. We have enough money to pay for everything we need, and we are able to save a little bit of money every month.

2 People who go to college usually have a higher **income** than people with only a high-school diploma.

3 Housing is the biggest **expenditure** for most people. Many Americans pay nearly 40% of their income in rent or house payments.

4 The weather is one **factor** that influences the price of food. For example, if there is not enough rain, crops are smaller and the price of food goes up.

5 Families with many children must spend a large **percentage** of their income on food and clothing.

6 It is a smart idea for workers to put some money into **savings** every month. Even $20 a month can grow into a large amount over time.

a ______________ (n) money that you put away, usually in a bank, for a later date

b ______________ (n) how much money and comfort someone has

c ______________ (n) one of the things that has an effect on a particular situation, decision, event, etc.

d ______________ (n) the total amount of money that a government or person spends on something

e ______________ (n) money that you earn by working, investing, or producing goods

f ______________ (n) an amount of something, expressed as a number out of 100

2 USING YOUR KNOWLEDGE **Work with a partner. Answer the questions, and explain your reasons.**

1 Do you think the standard of living in the United States has improved, gotten worse, or stayed the same in the last 20 years?

____

____

2 What factor or factors play an important role in determining people's standard of living?

____

____

3 SCANNING TO FIND INFORMATION **Scan the article on pages 150–151, and check your answers in Exercise 2.**

WHAT HAS HAPPENED TO THE AMERICAN DREAM?

1 One common definition of the "American Dream" is the belief that each generation will do better than the one before it. Unfortunately, many Americans today are not able to enjoy the same **standard of living** as their parents before them. The reason is that for the past 25 years, **incomes** have been declining while **expenditure** has been rising. In effect, this means many people are actually poorer than they were 20 years ago.

FALLING INCOMES

2 Falling incomes are the first cause of the declining standard of living. From 1945 to 1973, incomes increased by approximately 3% per year. From the mid-1970s to the mid-1990s, they continued to rise, though more slowly; but then they increased sharply between 1995 and 2000. Since 2000, however, incomes have been falling steadily. According to the U.S. Census Bureau, the median[1] income was $57,724 in 1999 and just $53,657 in 2014.

[1]**median** (adj) having a value that is exactly in the middle of a set of values arranged from largest to smallest

RISING EXPENDITURES

3 The other key **factor** in determining people's standard of living is expenditure. Figure 1 shows the **percentage** of their income that Americans spent on five key categories between 1996 and 2014: housing; food; transportation; pets, toys, and entertainment; and health. Until 2013, the costs for these five categories remained more or less stable. That is, Americans spent approximately 20% of their incomes on housing; about 10% on food; about 8% on transportation; and around 3% each for pets, toys, and entertainment; and health. As the graph shows clearly, except for pets, toys, and entertainment, all these costs jumped in 2013. By 2014, for instance, Americans were spending 25% of their income for housing and about 12% for food.

4 There are many reasons for rising expenditure over time, but two important ones are the high cost of housing and healthcare. In many cities, there is a critical shortage of houses and apartments to buy and rent. This has driven up costs. Also, healthcare costs have doubled since 1996 as prescription drugs and hospital costs have gotten more and more expensive. Transportation and food prices have also increased significantly in recent years.

5 In conclusion, the combination of rising prices and falling incomes has left many Americans with less spending power than they had 20 years ago. Because people must pay more for essentials like housing and food, they have less money for education, investment, savings, and small luxuries like eating in restaurants. Many people have had to sell their homes, use up their **savings**, or borrow money in order to meet their monthly expenditure. For these people, the American Dream must seem very far out of reach. Sadly, no one seems to know how or when the situation will improve.

Figure 1: U.S. Income and Expenditure, 1996–2014

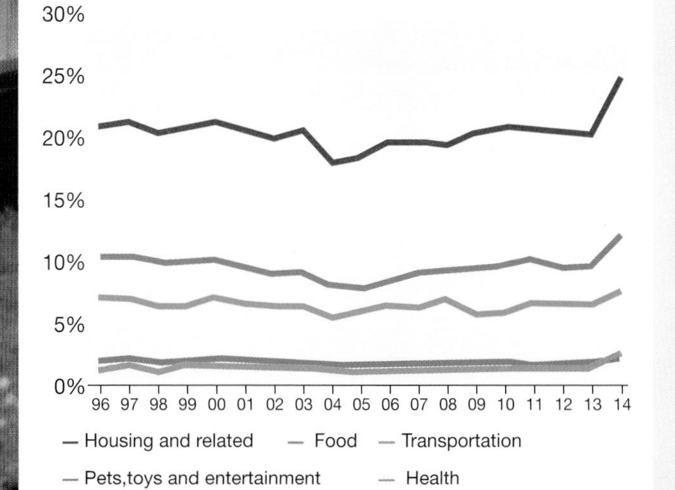

WHILE READING

4 ANNOTATING **Read and annotate the article on pages 150–151.**

5 READING FOR MAIN IDEAS **Choose the sentence that is the best summary of the article.**

a The article compares income and expenditure in the United States with the same factors in other developed countries.

b The article explains how falling incomes and rising expenditure have affected Americans' standard of living in recent years.

c The article describes five categories of expenditure that play a key role in determining people's standard of living.

SKILLS

UNDERSTANDING LINE GRAPHS

A line graph uses points on a line to show a trend. Use the following strategies to read and understand a line graph:

- Read the title. It gives the subject of the graph and often summarizes the most important trend that the data show.
- Look at the horizontal axis–the line that goes from left to right along the bottom. It usually shows the time period.
- Look at the vertical axis—the line that goes from top to bottom on the left side of the graph. This axis shows numbers or percentages.
- To "read" a line graph, notice the points where the vertical axis and horizontal axis meet. Each point tells you the number or percentage that matches one of the years along the bottom of the graph.
- Many line graphs have more than one line to show more than one trend. Each line will have a different color or pattern. Look for the legend—the box or sentence that explains what each color or pattern means.

6 TAKING NOTES **Look at Figure 1 on page 151 and complete the chart.**

subject	
horizontal axis	
vertical axis	
areas of expenditure	
general trend 1996–2012	
general trend 2013–2014	

7 READING FOR DETAILS **Read the article again and choose the correct statement from each pair.**

1 a Incomes rose quickly from 1995 to 2000, but they have been increasing very slowly since then.
  b Incomes rose quickly from 1995 to 2000, but they have been decreasing since then.

2 a Between 1999 and 2014, median income fell by about 7%.
  b Since 1999, median income in the U.S. has risen by about $4,000.00.

3 a Between 1996 and 2014, Americans spent more on transportation than they did on food.
  b Between 1996 and 2014, Americans' biggest expenditure was housing.

4 a Healthcare costs have stayed approximately the same in spite of rising hospital costs.
  b Because of higher prices for prescription drugs and hospital stays, healthcare costs have increased by about 100%.

READING BETWEEN THE LINES

8 MAKING INFERENCES **Work with a partner. Discuss the questions.**

1 Why are pets, toys, and entertainment combined into one group in the graph?
2 What could have caused the price of transportation to increase between 1996 and 2014?
3 If the average person earned around $53,600 in 2014, about how much did that person spend on housing?

CRITICAL THINKING

9 SYNTHESIZING **Work with a partner. Use ideas from Reading 1 and Reading 2 to answer the questions.**

APPLY

Do most Americans probably have more, less, or about the same amount of money to invest as they did 20 years ago? Why?

EVALUATE

If someone's income is falling and expenditure is rising, is it a good idea to try to make more money by investing? Why or why not?

COLLABORATION

10 **A** Work with a partner. What has happened to income and expenditure in your country in the last 20 years? Discuss the question. Then do research to see if you were correct.

B Repeat step A with a different country. Then compare the information for both countries.

C Present your information to the class. As a class, make a list of at least three general trends in the world in the last 20 years.

LANGUAGE DEVELOPMENT

NOUNS AND ADJECTIVES FOR ECONOMICS

1 Use a dictionary to find the meanings of the words in the chart.

noun	adjective
1 economy	economic
2 finance	financial
3 wealth	wealthy
4 poverty	poor
5 value	valuable
6 employment	employed
7 profession	professional
8 expense	expensive

2 Complete the sentences using either an adjective or a noun from the chart in Exercise 1.

1 Since 1999 the U.S. ______________ has been weak, with little growth.

2 Companies that are losing money often turn to the banks for ______________ assistance.

3 Only ______________ investors can afford to buy expensive classic cars.

4 As incomes have fallen in recent years, more and more Americans have fallen into ______________ .

5 Many wealthy people enjoy spending their money to buy ______________ art.

6 Each month, the U.S. government publishes the latest ______________ statistics on how many people have jobs.

7 ______________ services like legal or financial advice can cost a lot of money.

8 It is ______________ to buy even a single share in some successful companies, so you might want to start with companies whose shares cost a few dollars each.

NOUNS FOR ECONOMIC TRENDS

3 Read the definitions. Complete the sentences with the correct form of the words in bold.

consumer (n) a person who buys a product or service to use

demand (n) the need for something to be sold or supplied

market (n) the total number of people who might want to buy something

purchase (n) something that you buy

revenue (n) the income that a company or government receives

supply (n) an amount or quantity of something available to use

trend (n) the general direction of trends and developments

1 The ____________ for fast fashion is enormous in developed countries such as the United States, United Kingdom, and Japan.

2 I was not satisfied with my ____________ , so I returned the item to the store.

3 When shopping for large items like cars and refrigerators, smart ____________ compare prices before they make their decision.

4 A recent fashion ____________ for women is shoes with extremely high heels.

5 The company failed because there was not enough ____________ for the service it was selling.

6 ____________ from movie downloads has increased by more than 200% since 2010.

7 Prices go up when there is not enough ____________ of a product or service that people want.

WATCH AND LISTEN

GLOSSARY

stock market (n) a system for buying and selling stocks; the total value of all the investments that are traded in this system

crash (n) to fall or lose value suddenly and completely

depression (n) a period in which there is very little business activity and little employment

replica (n) a copy of an object

ticker tape (n) a long, thin strip of paper, used in the past for printing changing information on, for example, the prices of stocks

PREPARING TO WATCH

1 ACTIVATING YOUR KNOWLEDGE **Work with a partner. Discuss the questions.**

1 What cities in the world today are centers of finance?

2 What happens during an economic depression?

3 How healthy is the economy of your country?

2 PREDICTING CONTENT **You are going to watch a video about the Great Depression. Work with a partner. Use the photos from the video and your own knowledge to answer the questions.**

1 Where did it happen? ______________________________

2 When did it happen? ______________________________

3 How did it happen? ______________________________

4 Who did it affect? ______________________________

WHILE WATCHING

3 **Watch the video. Check your answers to Exercise 2.**

4 UNDERSTANDING MAIN IDEAS **Watch the video again. Match the sentence halves.**

1 The stock market
2 On Black Tuesday, investors
3 Millions of people
4 The Great Depression
5 Ticker tape machines

a was the worst economic period in modern history.
b were used to print the prices of stocks and shares.
c crashed in 1929.
d lost their jobs.
e lost billions of dollars.

5 UNDERSTANDING DETAILS **Watch the video again. Answer the questions.**

1 When did Black Tuesday happen? ______
2 Who was affected by the crash? ______
3 What happened to stock prices after Black Tuesday? ______
4 Where is the Museum of Financial History? ______
5 What does the stock exchange use now to report stock prices? ______

6 MAKING INFERENCES **Work with a partner. Discuss the questions and give reasons for your answers.**

1 Were most financial experts surprised by Black Tuesday?
2 Why did people in other countries lose their jobs during the Depression?
3 How have computers changed stock markets?

CRITICAL THINKING

7 **Work in a small group. Discuss your answers.**

APPLY
What are the biggest economic problems in the world today?

ANALYZE
How do changes in the economy affect your daily life?

ANALYZE
Do you think the economy will be better in ten years? Why or why not?

COLLABORATION

8 **A** Work in a small group. Research the Great Depression (1929–1941) or the Great Recession (2007–2009). Take notes on:

- the causes
- who was affected
- how they were affected
- how/why it ended
- what lessons were learned

B Present your research to the class. As a class, make lists of the similarities and the differences between the Great Depression and the Great Recession on the board.

GLOSSARY OF KEY VOCABULARY

Words that are part of the Academic Word List are noted with an (A) in this glossary.

UNIT 1 ANIMALS

READING 1

chemical (A) (n) man-made or natural substance made by changing atoms
destroy (v) to damage something very badly; to cause it to not exist
due to (prep) because of; as a result of
endangered (adj) (of plants and animals) that may disappear soon
natural (adj) as found in nature; not made or caused by people
pollute (v) to make an area or substance dirty and unhealthful
protect (v) to keep something or someone safe from damage or injury
species (n) types of plants or animals that have similar features

READING 2

common (adj) happening often or existing in large numbers
cruel (adj) causing pain or suffering on purpose
disease (n) illness; a serious health condition that requires care
fatal (adj) causing death
major (A) (adj) most serious or important
native (adj) used to describe animals and plants that grow naturally in a place
survive (A) (v) to continue to live after almost dying

UNIT 2 THE ENVIRONMENT

READING 1

atmosphere (n) the layer of air and gases around the Earth
cause (n) someone or something that makes something happen
climate (n) the general weather conditions usually found in a particular place
ecosystem (n) all the living things in an area and the effect they have on each other and the environment
fossil fuel (n) a source of energy like coal, gas, and petroleum, that was formed inside the Earth millions of years ago
global warming (n) an increase in the Earth's temperature because of pollution
greenhouse gas (n) a gas that makes the air around the Earth warmer
threaten (v) to be likely to damage or harm something

READING 2

absorb (v) to take in a liquid or gas, through a surface and hold it
construction (A) (n) the process of building something, usually large structures such as houses, roads, or bridges
destruction (n) the act of causing so much damage to something that it stops existing because it cannot be repaired
effect (n) result; a change that happens because of a cause
farming (n) the job of working on a farm or organizing work on a farm
logging (n) the activity or business of cutting down trees for wood
rainforest (n) a forest in a tropical area that gets a lot of rain

UNIT 3 TRANSPORTATION

READING 1

commuter (n) someone who travels between home and work or school regularly
connect (v) to join two things or places together
destination (n) the place where someone or something is going
outskirts (n) the outer area of a city or town
public transportation (n) a system of vehicles, such as buses and subways, which operate at regular times for public use
rail (adj) trains as a method of transportation
traffic congestion (n) when too many vehicles use a road network and it results in slower speeds or no movement at all

READING 2

cycle (v) to travel by bicycle
emergency (n) an unexpected situation that requires immediate action
engineering (n) the activity of designing and building things like bridges, roads, machines, etc.
fuel (n) a substance like gas or coal that produces energy when it is burned
government (n) the group of people that controls a country or city and makes decisions about laws, taxes, education, etc.
practical (adj) useful; suitable for the situation it is being used for
vehicle A (n) any machine that travels on roads, such as cars, buses, etc.

UNIT 4 CUSTOMS AND TRADITIONS

READING 1

appearance (n) the way someone or something looks
culture A (n) a society with its own ideas, traditions, and ways of behaving
exchange (v) to give something to someone, and receive something that they give you
expect (v) to think that something will or should happen
formal (adj) correct or conservative in style, dress, or speech; not casual
greet (v) to welcome someone with particular words or actions
relationship (n) the way two people or groups feel and behave toward each other

READING 2

belief (n) an idea that you are certain is true
ceremony (n) a formal event with special traditions, activities, or words, such as a wedding
couple A (n) two people who are married or in a relationship
engaged (adj) having a formal agreement to get married
reception (n) a formal party that is given to celebrate a special event or to welcome someone
relative (n) any member of your family
theme A (n) the main idea, subject, or topic of an event, book, musical piece, etc.

UNIT 5 HEALTH AND FITNESS

READING 1

active (adj) doing things that involve movement and energy
calorie (n) measurement of the amount of energy found in food
moderate (adj) not too much and not too little
recognize (v) to understand; to accept that something is true
reduce (v) to limit; to use less of something
self-esteem (n) a feeling of confidence and pride in yourself
serious (adj) bad or dangerous

READING 2

balanced diet (n) a daily eating program that has a healthy mixture of different kinds of food
campaign (n) a group of activities designed to motivate people to take action, such as giving money or changing their behavior
junk food (n) food that is unhealthy but quick and easy to eat
nutritional (adj) relating to food and the way it affects your health
obesity (n) the condition of being extremely overweight
portion A (n) an amount of food served to one person

UNIT 6 DISCOVERY AND INVENTION

READING 1

essential (adj) very important or necessary
harmful (adj) able to hurt or damage
helpful (adj) useful
illustrate A (v) to show the meaning or truth of something more clearly, especially by giving examples
pattern (n) a set of lines, colors, or shapes that repeat in a regular way
prevent (v) to stop something from happening or stop someone from doing something
unlimited (adj) without end or restriction

READING 2

artificial (adj) not natural; made by people
break down (phr v) to stop working
electronic (adj) sent or accessed by means of a computer or other electronic device
movement (n) a change of position or place
object (n) a thing you can see or touch that isn't alive
personal (adj) belonging or used by just one person
power (n) energy, usually electricity, used to provide heat, light, etc.
three-dimensional (adj) not flat; having depth, length, and width

UNIT 7 FASHION

READING 1

brand (n) the name of a product or group of products made by a company
collection (n) a group of new clothes produced by a fashion house
cotton (n) a plant with white fibers used for making cloth
invest A (v) to use money for the purpose of making a profit, for example, by building a factory
manufacture (v) to make goods in a large quantity in a factory
season (n) a time of year when particular things happen
volume A (n) amount of something, especially when it is large

READING 2

conditions (n) the physical environment where people live or work
import (v) to buy a product from another country and bring it into your country
multinational (adj) referring to a business or company that has offices, stores, or factories in several countries
offshore (adj) located in another country
outsource (v) to have work done by another company, often in another country, rather than in your own company
textile (n) cloth or fabric that is made by crossing threads under and over each other
wage (n) money that people earn for working

UNIT 8 ECONOMICS

READING 1

interest rate (n) the percentage amount that you pay when you borrow money, or receive when you lend money, for a period of time
investment A (n) something such as stocks, bonds, or property that you buy in order to make a profit
investor A (n) someone who puts money in a bank, business, etc. to make a profit
recession (n) a period when the economy of a country is not doing well
return (n) profit on an investment
stocks and shares (n) parts of a publicly owned business that can be bought and sold
value (n) how much money something could be sold for

READING 2

expenditure (n) the total amount of money that a government or person spends on something
factor A (n) one of the things that has an effect on a particular situation, decision, event, etc.
income A (n) money that you earn by working, investing, or producing goods
percentage A (n) an amount of something, expressed as a number out of 100
savings (n) money that you put away, usually in a bank, for a later date
standard of living (n) how much money and comfort someone has

VIDEO SCRIPTS

UNIT 1

Great Egret and Dolphin Fishing Teamwork

The marshes of South Carolina are the location of an interesting fish tale.
There, these dolphins and egrets work together in a very special way.
These egrets are experts on the dolphins' behavior.
The moment a dolphin comes to the surface of the water and checks the nearest mud bank, the birds get ready for action.
Then, it happens. The dolphins push the fish onto the shore.
When the fish are out of the water, the dolphins start eating. But the egrets also join them for dinner.
This is the only place in the world where you can see this kind of behavior.
Strangely, the dolphins always use their right sides to push the fish to the shore.
The young dolphins learn this fishing technique from their parents, and so do the young egrets. Many of the birds now depend on the dolphins for their food. They never even fish for themselves. These egrets and dolphins demonstrate the ability of different animal species to work together in order to survive.

UNIT 2

Colorado River, Grand Canyon, Yosemite

Some of the world's most beautiful natural environments are in the southwestern United States.
In just a few million years, the Colorado River has cut through parts of Arizona to form the Grand Canyon.
The Grand Canyon is 277 miles long and, in some places, 18 miles wide. At its deepest places, the river is a mile below the top of the canyon. It shows the effects of water and weather on the Earth's surface.
Its oldest rocks are almost 2 billion years old, nearly half the age of the Earth. This is the world's largest canyon, and the weather here can change dramatically. In the same day you can have hot, dry weather, followed by wind and snow. And every year the Colorado River cuts a little deeper into the bottom of the Grand Canyon.
Water also formed Carlsbad Caverns in New Mexico. Carlsbad is the largest, deepest cave system in North America. Even today water continues to change the inside of the caves.
The results are spectacular.
Finally, high in the Sierra Mountains of California is Yosemite National Park. Its famous landmark Half Dome was made by the frozen water in a glacier moving through the canyon.
Today the glaciers are gone, but water from the melting mountain snow flows throughout the national park.
Yosemite Falls drops nearly 2,500 feet—it's the tallest waterfall in North America.

UNIT 3

The Jumbo Jet

Narrator: In 1969, a true giant of the skies first took flight. It could cross the Atlantic with enough fuel and twice as many passengers as any airplane before it. Now, there are nearly 1,000 of them. Each one is able to fly over 14 hours to their destinations without stopping. It's

the 747—the jumbo jet—and this is the very first one.
Jimmy Barber helped build this very plane.

Jimmy Barber: Eight months straight you worked on the airplane, and we didn't just work, err, eight hours a day. Sometimes we worked 12 or more hours a day. And if it was necessary to sleep in your car in a parking lot, that's what you did. It was a highlight in my whole life was this aircraft, you know. Yeah. Wow, this is great.

Narrator: This is the first time Jimmy has been aboard since he worked on it over 45 years ago.

Jimmy Barber: This is great.

Narrator: When it first flew, this was the most modern plane in the air. It was the first double-decker jet in history with a fancy first-class lounge upstairs.

Jimmy Barber: And the upper deck, one airline turned that into a disco and put a dance floor up there. Another airline put piano bars in his … in these airplanes.

Narrator: But it was the enormous space downstairs that changed commercial air travel forever. With room for around 500 people, it started the age of low-cost air travel.
Since its first flight, engineers have redesigned the 747 fifteen times. Today it flies further and faster than ever before

UNIT 4

Halloween by the Numbers

Now, a little Halloween by the numbers. Tens of millions of trick-or-treaters are expected to hit the streets tomorrow. We purchase an estimated 600 million pounds of candy for Halloween, and if you haven't gotten to it yet, we are told that the most popular variety is—no surprise—chocolate. Other top costume choices include witches, pirates, and Batman. More than a billion pounds of pumpkins were grown last year. Illinois is the nation's number one pumpkin producing state. As for the origin of trick-or-treating, it is thought to have evolved from a Celtic tradition of putting out treats to placate the spirits who roam the streets during a sacred festival that marked the end of the Celtic year. Finally, you may be surprised to learn that there is nothing frightening about Halloween if you are a retailer. It is the second highest grossing holiday after Christmas. The National Retail Federation estimates the average person will spend nearly $75 on decorations, costumes and, of course, candy.

UNIT 5

Nutrition Labels

Reporter: Today the Food and Drug Administration proposed a food label makeover. Jeff Pegues tells us it includes a reality check that some feel is long overdue.

Jeff Pegues: What and how people eat have changed. Now, for the first time in two decades, the labels on foods will change, too. The calories will be featured more prominently, and any added sugars or sweeteners will be listed as well. FDA commissioner Margaret Hamburg.

Margaret Hamburg: We're also asking for a change in serving size to reflect the realities of what people are eating.

Jeff Pegues: Here's what that means. The label on this pint of Ben & Jerry's chocolate chip cookie dough ice cream says each halfcup serving has 280 calories and 25% of the fat we should eat every day. Under the FDA proposal, the serving size would be a more realistic cup, which means each serving would contain 560 calories and 50% fat. At least publically, the food and beverage industry has been supportive. The Grocery Manufacturers Association says it's critical that any changes ultimately serve to inform and not confuse consumers. Some beverage companies, like PepsiCo, have already made changes, but what may be difficult for the industry to swallow, the overall price tag. A senior Obama administration official says the cost of implementing the changes could reach 2 billion dollars. First Lady Michelle Obama is a driving force behind the new labels.

Michelle Obama: As consumers and as parents, we have a right to understand what's in the food we're feeding our families, because that's really the only way that we can make informed choices.

Reporter: This is just a proposal, so there will be a public comment period. Nora, the FDA says it may be two years before consumers see these new labels on food in stores.

UNIT 6

China's Man-made River

History is filled with stories of humans overcoming obstacles through discovery and invention. Take an enormous country like China. What do you do when most of your people live in the north, in cities like Beijing, but most of your water is in the south? You build an artificial river to bring water from the south to the north.

This river will be about 750 miles long when it is finished in 2030.

And this is it. A giant raised canal, or aqueduct—one of the largest engineering projects in the world.

Chinese workers and engineers are building the river piece by piece, in separate sections.

Each section starts as a metal framework.

A team of 20 people build the metal frame.

Then the concrete is added.

Finally, the section is moved into place using one of the world's most powerful cranes.

Each section weighs 1,200 tons—more than three commercial airplanes.

This woman operates the crane. It's a very important job, and it takes great skill.

She must work very carefully so that each section of the artificial river is in the perfect position.

The water will flow north to Beijing without using any pumps.

So the end of each section must be exactly 1 centimeter lower than the other end.

When the river is finished and operating in 2030, the water from the south will reach millions of Chinese people in the north.

UNIT 7

A Life Tailored Around Clothes

Edgar Pomeroy: I'm Edgar Pomeroy. I grew up in Savannah, Georgia, and I knew I wanted to be a fashion designer when I was ten years old. Well, every day I used to watch my father get dressed because I would be watching cartoons or something on TV in their bedroom. And he was always putting on pinstripe suits and polka-dot ties and waistcoats and dressed to the nines, as they say. He was the only one I've ever known to mow the lawn in a Brooks Brothers button-down and khaki pants, and Weejuns, might I add. That's really how it all began.

Father: But you've always been able to put fabrics and colors together.

Edgar Pomeroy: Yeah, but look who I'm talking to. We're bespoke tailors as well as I'm more of a designer so we make our shirts and suits and all our clothes right here. We don't source anything out. This is for a client that I'm seeing tomorrow.
All the stripes match. The plaids come down. This is detail.
I'm upstairs when I'm in town pretty much all the time, checking the jackets and pants and seeing who's doing what. It has to fit. You can do the most beautiful cloth in the world but if you botch the cutting, it's over.
It's just another piece of cloth that should be burned up in the floor. It got very lackadaisical in the 90s when the dot-com era came into play. And I was kind of disappointed because people kind of started dressing way down. Some even looked like they just mowed their lawn. I dress people who love clothes. People who want to stand out, elegantly, of course.
But they're dandies.
I didn't want to overkill this because you're conservative.
I go to their houses in Chicago, I go to L.A., I go to Baltimore, New York, London. I go all over. You know, I build a trust with them and I design for them. What I do is get to know their personality. If I go to their office or home, I look around, I see how it's decorated, I look at pictures, and I design around their personality. But I want them to take a little bit of a step out of their comfort zone. A little one, just to try. I let the client have the stage. I just kind of help them get to the stage.

UNIT 8

Stock Market Crash of 1929

Narrator: On October 29, 1929, the New York Stock Exchange had its worst day ever—Black Tuesday. The stock market crashed, and investors lost billions of dollars in a single day. That day was the end of a decade of a strong U.S economy. It was the beginning of the Great Depression, the worst economic period in modern world history. During the next two years, stock prices fell 90%, banks and companies failed, and millions of people around the world lost their jobs.
Today you can visit the Museum of Financial History on Wall Street, in New York City, to learn more about what happened.

Man: So what we have here is the physical tape from October 29th, that Black Tuesday, and it's quite an important piece, it tells a great story.

Narrator: This is a replica of the machine that produced that ticker tape. The name *ticker tape* comes from the sound of the machine as it printed out the price of stocks and shares. But since the early 1970s, computers and electronic boards have reported the ups and downs in the stock market.

CREDITS

Photo credits

The publishers are grateful to the following for permission to reproduce copyright photographs and material

Key: T = Top, C = Center, B = Below, L = Left, R = Right, TL = Top Left, TR = Top Right, BL = Below Left, BR = Below Right, CL = Center Left, CR = Center Right, BG = Background

The following images are sourced from Getty Images.

pp. 14-15: Brian Mckay Photographyy/Moment; p. 16 (TL): Naphat Photography/Moment; p. 16 (BL): Bill Brooks/Moment; p. 16 (TR): Jrg Weimann/Eyeem; p. 16 (BR): Holly Harris/Stone; p. 16 (BG): David Fettes/Cultura; p. 17: Gabrielle Therin-Weise; pp. 18-19: Alex Stoen Photography/Moment; p. 19 (BL): Paula French/Eyeem; p. 19 (BC): Dougal Waters/The Image Bank; p. 19 (BR): M Swiet Productions/Moment; p. 21: Michael Hevesy/Photolibrary; pp. 22-23: Andrea Pistolesi/Photolibrary; p. 23 (TL): Pierre Longnus; p. 23 (CL): Gerard Soury/Oxford Scientific; p. 23 (TR): Mattpaul/Room; p. 23 (CR): Jialiang Gao/Moment; p. 23 (BL): Ben Queenborough/Oxford Scientific; p. 23 (BR): James Warwick/The Image Bank; p. 24 (T): Pauline Lewis/Moment; p. 24 (BR): Alexturton/Moment; p. 25 (BR): Stuart Shore/Wight Wildlfie Photography; p. 27: Westend61; pp. 28-29: Tuul/Bruno Morandi/Photolibrary; p. 30: M Swiet Productions/Moment; p. 31: Nick Rains; pp. 32-33: Janmiko/Istock; pp. 34-35: Wu Swee Ong/Moment; p. 34 (TL): Qai Publishing/Universal Images Group; p. 34 (TR): Bsip/Universal Images Group; p. 34 (TC): Simon Dawson/Bloomberg; pp. 36-37: Maximilian Müller/Moment; p. 37 (BL): Abadonian/Istock; p. 37 (BC): Ashley Cooper/Corbis Documentary; p. 37 (BR): Danita Delimont/Gallo Images; p. 39: Rainervonbrandis/Istock; p. 40: Australian Scenics/Photolibrary; p. 41: Panoramic Images; p. 42: Minden Pictures; p. 43: Jacques Jangoux/Visuals Unlimited, Inc.; p. 47: Jeff Krause Photography/Moment; p. 48: Ted Soqui/Corbis Historical; pp. 50-51: Altrendo Travel/Juice Images; p. 52: Michael Wheatley/All Canada Photos; p. 53: Kevork Djansezian; pp. 54-55: Fototrav/Vetta; p. 54 (BL): Tony Burns/Lonely Planet Images; p. 55 (TR): Gary John Norman/Photolibrary; p. 55 (BR): Hufton And Crow/View/Passage; pp. 56-57: Extreme Photographer/Istock; p. 58 (BL): Michael Short/Bloomberg; p. 58 (BR): Maskot; p. 59: Ullstein Bild; p. 60: Bernie Dechant/Photonica; p. 61 (C): Pastorscott/E+; p. 61 (CL): Gavin Hellier/Robertharding; p. 61 (CR): Don Emmert/Afp; pp. 62-63: Thomas Northcut/Digitalvision; p. 64: Charles Bowman/Photolibrary; p. 65: Zoran Milich/Photonica; p. 66: Artur Widak/Nurphoto; pp. 68-69: Www.Jethuynh.Com/Moment; p. 70: Hugh Sitton/Corbis; p. 71: Kidstock/Blend Images; p. 72: Allan Danahar/Photodisc; p. 73 (CR): Imagesbazaar; p. 73 (TR): Pavliha/E+; pp. 76-77: Jose Fuste Raga/Corbis Documentary; p. 78 (T): John Phillips/Uk Press; p. 78 (BR): Jumaydesigns/Istock; p. 79 (CR): Tommaso Boddi/Wireimage; p. 79 (TL): Jeremy Woodhouse/Blend Images; p. 81: Waseem Gashroo/Hindustan Times; p. 84: Ariel Skelley/The Image Bank; pp. 86-87: Piola666/E+; pp. 88-89: Ryan Creary/All Canada Photos; p. 89 (a): Michael Heffernan/Taxi; p. 89 (b): Image Source; p. 89 (c): Kathrin Ziegler/Taxi; p. 89 (d): Resolution Productions/Blend Images; p. 89 (e): Ariel Skelley/Brand X Pictures; p. 89 (f): Viktorcap/Istock; p. 89 (g): Westend61; p. 89 (h): Tom M Johnson/Blend Images; pp. 90-91: Paul Bradbury/Caiaimage/Riser; p. 91 (CL): Pawel Libera/LightRocket; p. 91 (CR): Jade/Blend Images; p. 94: Fatcamera/E+; p. 95: Firina/Istock; p. 96: Madeline Dudley-Yates/Eyeem; p. 97 (TR): Steinar Lund/Ikon Images; p. 97 (BL): Steve Prezant/Blend Images; p. 100: Ariel Skelley/Blend Images; p. 102: Moodboard; pp. 104-105: Caiaimage/Agnieszka Olek; pp. 106-107: Mint Images; p. 107 (CL): Nacivet/Photographer'S Choice; p. 107 (CR): Danita Delimont/Gallo Images; p. 108: Cormacmccreesh/Room; p. 109 (TL): Clouds Hill Imaging Ltd./Corbis Documentary; p. 109 (BR): Alex Wong News; p. 109 (TR): Andrew Holt; p. 109 (CR): Anthony Renaud/Eyeem; p. 111 (BL): Mark Hughes/Moment; p. 111 (BR): Kokoroimages.Com/Moment; p. 113: Terrafugia/Barcroft Cars/Barcroft Media; p. 114: Victor Habbick/Visuals Unlimited; p. 115 (BL): Izabela Habur/E+; p. 115 (BR): Koichi Kamoshida News; p. 120: Keren Su/China Span; pp. 122-123: Westend61; pp. 124-125: Chelsea Lauren Entertainment; p. 125: Peopleimages/Digitalvision; p. 126: Timothy Hiatt Entertainment; p. 127 (TL): Ahmet Bolat/Anadolu Agency; p. 127 (spot): Mangostock/Istock; p. 127 (spot): Jetta Productions/Blend Images; p. 127 (spot): Atsushi Yamada/The Image Bank; p. 127 (spot): Goodluz/Istock; p. 127 (spot): Jacob Wackerhausen/Istock; p. 127 (spot): Eugenio Marongiu/Cultura; pp. 128-129: Jon Boyes/Canopy; p. 130: Erik Isakson/Blend Images; p. 131: Munir Uz Zaman/Afp; p. 132: Danita Delimont/Gallo Images; p. 133: Christopher Pillitz/Photonica World; p. 136: Alexander Spatari/Moment; p. 137: Arthur Morris/Corbis Documentary; p. 138: Hxdbzxy/Istock; pp. 140-141: Hero Images; p. 143: Brian Lawrence/The Image Bank; p. 144: Yodiyim/Istock; p. 145: Heritage Images/Hulton Archive; p. 146: Car Culture; p. 147: Jan Cobb Photography Ltd/Photographer'S Choice; p. 148: Comstock Images/Stockbyte; p. 149: Cameron Davidson/Photographer'S Choice; p. 150 (T): Ariel Skelley/Digitalvision; p. 150 (BR): Marianna Massey/Digitalvision; p. 151: Gary D Ercole/Photolibrary; p. 155: Bryan R. Smith/Afp; p. 156: Siegfried Layda/Photographer'S Choice.

Video Supplied by BBC Worldwide Learning.

Video Stills Supplied by BBC Worldwide Learning.

Corpus

Development of this publication has made use of the Cambridge English Corpus (CEC). The CEC is a multi-billion word computer database of contemporary spoken and written English. It includes British English, American English, and other varieties of English. It also includes the Cambridge Learner Corpus, developed in collaboration with the University of Cambridge ESOL Examinations. Cambridge University Press has built up the CEC to provide evidence about language use that helps produce better language teaching materials.

Cambridge Dictionaries

Cambridge dictionaries are the world's most widely used dictionaries for learners of English. The dictionaries are available in print and online at dictionary.cambridge.org. Copyright © Cambridge University Press, reproduced with permission.

Typeset by QBS

Audio by John Marshall Media

INFORMED BY TEACHERS

Classroom teachers shaped everything about *Prism*. The topics. The exercises. The critical thinking skills. Everything. We are confident that *Prism* will help your students succeed in college because teachers just like you helped guide the creation of this series.

Prism Advisory Panel

The members of the *Prism* Advisory Panel provided inspiration, ideas, and feedback on many aspects of the series. *Prism* is stronger because of their contributions.

Gloria Munson
University of Texas, Arlington

Kim Oliver
Austin Community College

Wayne Gregory
Portland State University

Julaine Rosner
Mission College

Dinorah Sapp
University of Mississippi

Christine Hagan
George Brown College/Seneca College

Heidi Lieb
Bergen Community College

Stephanie Kasuboski
Cuyahoga Community College

GLOBAL INPUT

Teachers from more than 500 institutions all over the world provided valuable input through:

- Surveys
- Focus Groups
- Reviews